ROYAL BLOODLINE WETIKO
&
THE GREAT REMEMBERING

DEAN HENDERSON

Royal Bloodline Wetiko & The Great Remembering

Copyright © 2023 Dean Henderson. All rights reserved.

Editing, cover, cover photo and interior design: Jill Henderson

All rights reserved. No part of this book, either in part or in whole, may be reproduced, transmitted or utilized in any form or by any means, electronic, photographic or mechanical, including photocopying, recording, or by any information storage and retrieval system, without permission in writing from the Author or his heirs, except for brief quotations embodied in literary articles and reviews.

ISBN: 9798372433731

DEDICATION

An ode to Harvey Wall Banger (Fozzy Bear), Silent Bob (Honey Bear) and Slow Loris (Pudding Bear) who kept me grounded in the love and beauty of the natural world as the screens rolled out and the humans rolled over.

TABLE OF CONTENTS

Introduction: Death of a Monarch, Birth of a Revolution

Chapter 1: Crazy Horse

Chapter 2: Slow Loris

Chapter 3: Wakan Tanka and the Good Red Road

Chapter 4: The Anunnaki Bloodline: From Sumeria to Egypt

Chapter 5: The Unholy Roman Empire

Chapter 6: The City of London

Chapter 7: Farming Humanity

Chapter 8: The East India Company: Slavery, Opium and Adam Smith

Chapter 9: Hobbes, Malthus, and Locke

Chapter 10: The Royal Society

Chapter 11: First-Strike Wetiko

Chapter 12: The Bloodline Take Down of America: Part I

Chapter 13: The Royal Command Structure

Chapter 14: Neocolonialism

Chapter 15: Crown Deception Becomes Public Perception

Chapter 16: The Royal Alchemist Assault on Humanity

Chapter 17: The Bloodline Take Down of America: Part II

Chapter 18: The Internet/Social Media Reveal

Chapter 19: Manufacturing the Two-Party Cult

Chapter 20: Wokism and Hive Mind Singularity

Chapter 21: COVID-19 and The Great Reset

Chapter 22: Stockholm Syndrome

Chapter 23: The Great Remembering

Chapter 24: Slow Loris Returns to the Land of Crazy Horse

Introduction

Death of a Monarch, Birth of a Revolution

The Cree used the word *wetiko* to describe a cannibal. But it means much more than "one who devours flesh". It means one who devours life itself, who seeks to devour your soul.

In the real world, it is plausible that the death of a wetiko monarch could symbolize the end of an epoch and could usher in a global revolution based not so much on a mass awakening as on a collective remembering.

Of course, the media (based on the Latin word "medium") does its very best to do what a medium does and that is to get in between you and the real world, making sure through this crucial magical process that you have no such thoughts regarding the matter. This, however, would constitute a virtual reality as opposed to the real world.

Instead, the death of Queen Elizabeth II in late 2022 was sold to the public as a time to grieve the passing of the world's largest landowner whose self-declared 8,500-year-old royal bloodline has enslaved, farmed, industrialized, commercialized, atomized, objectified, raped, pillaged, tortured, murdered and finally controlled the very minds of humanity.

In the real world, it is plausible that humanity would have largely seen right through the what seemed to be never-ending media coverage of this ritual black mass, meant to mesmerize the peasantry with it's close-up photos of the crowns, jewels and seals, symbolizing the power which this one single bloodline usurped, then weaponized against humanity when King Sargon became this world's first "royal monarch" in Sumeria those few short eight-thousand five-hundred years ago.

Naturally, the mediums, whose now plummeting stock is owned by these same shrewd, but not very bright, bloodline magicians, have neglected to inform their viewers/readers/mind-control subjects of the true history of this bloodline. But surely even the most severely bamboozled prole must have noticed that for a gaggle that supposedly "has no real power", it sure was a long funeral.

Herein, we shall explore not only the events that have transpired during the brutal reign of these planetary usurpers. But more importantly, we will examine the lies that they have inculcated in their human subjects. For it is chiefly these well-entrenched lies about the nature of reality which prevent us from remembering who we are. Once we remember, these self-appointed fake gods will be easily deposed and humanity can experience a revolution from the subjugation, bondage, oppression, poverty, and environmental degradation they have wrought.

They know we are beginning to remember. Soon the masses may even translate "Deep State" into Crown, which is more accurate and precise. Thus, the extended black mass mind-control charade to put us back to sleep during the queen's week's-long funeral.

Current geopolitical events are keeping them up at night. They poked the Russian bear, then provoked the Chinese dragon in an attempt to keep their economic Ponzi scheme afloat. Their Fourth Industrial Revolution AI cloud pipe dream is wobbly at best, so they've pivoted back to their old military-industrial footing. The Crown has been embroiled in scandal after scandal of late. When cornered, these are dangerous creatures, since they have the militaries of entire countries at their disposal.

But we the people have the numbers. We always have. All we have to do is remember what happened to us and find out who did it so that we can hold them accountable. I've spent most of my adult life refining the identities of these perpetrators and my first six books reflect that research. In the end, my conclusion is that this single royal bloodline, which includes the kings, queens, princes, princesses, dukes, lords, viscounts, earls, sirs, sultans, sheiks and knights in every single country in the world retrograde enough to recognize them, is ultimately behind every genocide, war, slave trade, famine, plague and environmental catastrophe our world has experienced since their arrival on the scene in Sumeria 8,500 years ago.

Once we know the real history of our world we can remember the truth and begin to live in the real world rather than accepting the media-driven virtual reality deception that their programmers present to us, a phenomenon which has only intensified with the advent of television and the more recent arrival of the internet and "smart" phones.

So now is our time. We are at a major crossroads. The time for fence-sitting is over. Either we expose this bloodline and all its tentacles and depose it, or we expose ourselves, our families, our children, and our natural world to their deadly response to our remembering, which has recently intensified and will continue to do so.

Or as the great Lakota warrior Crazy Horse once said, "It is a good day to die".

Chapter 1

Crazy Horse

A massive stone carving of Tȟašúŋke Witkó points south over the Black Hills (*Paha Sapa*) of western South Dakota towards the place that his people had thrived, gone to battle, and died fighting Crown-funded invaders drunk with the discovery of gold.

Crazy Horse told his Lakota family that he would return to them in stone. Thanks to Polish sculptor Korczak Ziolkowski, who was commissioned by Lakota elder Henry Standing Bear to carve the image of Crazy Horse into a chunk of Paha Sapa granite, he has. I stood just inches away from his giant stone lips on one of the last days of September 2020. And I listened.

These words emerged from that very sentient rock.

"Be strong. Be brave. Be quiet."

Crazy Horse came into the world in 1840 as swarms of wetiko settlers tumbled west like weeds, intoxicated with Crown-inspired nightmares of conquest, land ownership, materialism, and expediency.

Although he was killed while still a young man by a US Army soldier in 1877 at Fort Robinson, Nebraska, Crazy Horse remains a legend. He knew exactly what he was trying to stop and he didn't need any Crown-funded history books to inform him on the matter.

As John Neihardt noted in *Black Elk Speaks*, Crazy Horse was "...a queer man and would go about the village without noticing people or saying anything. In his own tipi he would joke, and when he was on the warpath with a small party, he would joke to make his warriors feel good. But around the village he hardly ever noticed anybody, except little children. All the Lakota like to dance and sing; but he never joined a dance, and they say nobody ever heard him sing. But everybody liked him, and they would do anything he wanted or go anywhere he said."

The US government had been busy crafting treaties, using the "Queen's English" to trick Native Americans across the continent into relinquishing their land. When that failed there were always mercenary Indian killers like Daniel Boone, Kit Carson, and Davy Crockett to be deployed. By using these types of "irregular scouts" the US government, in cahoots with the Crown's corporate appendages, could absolve themselves of the genocide.

The inter-mountain West was the last bastion of Native people living naturally in what is now the United States. The Shoshone, Arapaho, Cheyenne, Crow and Sioux occupied this land which encompassed parts of Wyoming, North and South Dakota, Montana, Colorado and Utah. It was not until around the time of Thašúŋke Witkó's birth that the colonial invaders reached this last sanctuary for indigenous people in North America.

These tribes had gotten word of the ongoing genocide working its way from both the Atlantic and Pacific Oceans. They were thus more leery and more militant than their coastal cousins in their attitudes towards the Wašíču. Still, like the real human beings they were, the tribes desired peace. In 1868, they signed the Treaty of Fort Laramie.

This granted the tribes a huge swath of territory bordered to the north and east by the Missouri River, to the south by the North Platte River and to the west by the Tongue River. Included in this area, the treaty granted the Lakota Sioux people the Paha Sapa of western South Dakota and eastern Wyoming.

But in 1874 an expedition led by General George Armstrong Custer discovered gold in the Black Hills. Two years later in 1876 the Congressional forked tongues in Washington signed the misnamed Indian Appropriations Bill, which, without the consent of the Lakota, revoked the Fort Laramie Treaty promise of the Paha Sapa in favor of the Crown's Homestake gold mining interests, controlled by the San Francisco-based Hearst family.

One-hundred fifty-six Lakota signed the Treaty, including important leaders such as Sitting Bull, Red Cloud, and American Horse. Crazy Horse had refused to sign. He never trusted the Wašíču and instead chose the fight them at every turn. His bravery and record of military victories against the US Army earned him the name *Ogle Tanka Un* or "shirt-wearer" among his people. This made him the de facto military leader of the Lakota.

On December 21, 1866, Crazy Horse led an ambush on US troops at the base of the Big Horn Mountains in Wyoming. All eighty-one soldiers were killed in what was the worst defeat for Washington since the Indian Wars began. It became known as the Fetterman Massacre.

On June 17, 1876 Crazy Horse led 1,500 Lakota and Northern Cheyenne warriors in a surprise attack on 1,000 US Cavalry troops under the command of General George Crook in what became known as the Battle of the Rosebud. The attack delayed Crook's arrival at Little Big Horn where his troops were to join those led by General George Armstrong Custer.

One week late, as Custer's 7th Cavalry attacked a Lakota/Cheyenne encampment at Little Big Horn in eastern Montana, Crazy Horse exhorted his fellow warriors into battle crying, *Hóka-héy!* (onward towards the danger). It is a good day to die!" He led a group of Lakota fighters who flanked Custer's troops and delivered the only major victory ever recorded by the Native American resistance against Uncle Sam's Army.

Frustrated by the stubborn success of Crazy Horse, the Army invited him to Fort Robinson in western Nebraska for negotiations. He arrived there in good faith on May 5, 1877. Four months later negotiations broke down and he was placed under arrest. Refusing to be jailed, he resisted by pulling a knife. A soldier stuck a bayonet in his back and Crazy Horse was dead.

Though the location of his grave has been kept secret, I am told he is buried in the South Dakota Badlands. He was one of the bravest men to ever walk this earth. And his words to me in September 2020 at the Crazy Horse Monument south of Hill City were clear. "Be strong. Be brave. Be quiet".

Of those three revelations the one that stood out the most was the last. As to the first two, I had spent the better part of these past decades confronting the evil that has transformed our beautiful natural world into a slave plantation. My research progressed from corporations to banks to families to the Nephilim Crown/City of London. The order in which my six previous books were written reflects a honing in on the exact identity of the parasite that feeds off of us and hoards that which Wakan Tanka made for all of us.

Still alive and well after assassination attempts, perpetual surveillance and most recently, a banishment from the Crown's internet operation; I was feeling pretty good in the bravery department.

We had sold our Missouri Ozarks farm in November 2019 and moved to the Paha Sapa stronghold just before the Crown's COVID-19 (Covert Identification 2019) military operation began. Here we focused on hiking, swimming, and exercise of the non-work type. I had gained ten pounds, found a good chiropractor to straighten my overworked skeleton and now feel as fit as I have in years. So I was feeling that the strength aspect was moving along quite nicely. But what of the quiet?

How can one win a war against evil by staying quiet? I had been under the impression that all revolutions were messy, noisy, chaotic affairs. I have always tended to side with the more militant approach to taking down these parasites.

But beneath the surface and upon deeper reflection, even a battle-hardened revolutionary must stay calm and grounded, especially in the midst of the battle. In the end, these are the very characteristics of the royal bloodline we are fighting. They are clinically insane, or wetiko, as the Arapaho say.

So, in a very real sense, in order to depose them we must remain rational, calm, and quiet. A lesson that nature provides us every day if we live in the real world rather than the hurried virtual world that the Crown is currently working overtime to subject us to. Sure, there is the occasional tornado, hurricane, or tropical downpour, but in general, things in nature move at a very slow and methodical pace.

For me, that lesson as to the nature of reality is provided daily by a very special cat.

Chapter 2

Slow Loris

Accompanying my wife and me on our journey to the Paha Sapa stronghold was a giant cat named Slow Loris. We went rock to rock, from the ground-down ancient limestone respite of the Missouri Ozarks to the oft-pulverized and even older granite spires of the Black Hills of South Dakota.

Less than a year after we moved into our Ozarks redoubt, a mamma cat we named Boots spent a couple of days sussing us out before bringing two of her kittens onto our front porch. Half-starved and ragged, Boots eventually decided we were the ones who should look after them. We named these two male kittens Harvey Wall Banger and Silent Bob for reasons that were immediately obvious.

That night at 2:00 AM we were awakened by the cry of a kitten on our back porch. I turned on the outside light expecting to see Bob or Harvey, only to catch a glimpse of a third kitten bolting for the woods. After spending the entire next day, and using Boots as bait, we finally persuaded this third more leery kitten to come into the front porch fold. His name, for even more obvious reasons, would be Slow Loris.

Shortly after we neutered and wormed them all Boots took off, leaving her kittens to be raised by us. When the chill of fall came we caved in and let them in the house at night. Soon they were spending most of their days there as well. And for the next five years we became a family.

They were loved equally and each was unique in personality, laying bare the Crown lie that who we are is simply the result of either nature or nurture. Though they all had the same genetics and were raised in the same environment, their spirits were all so very different. They each had their own unique soul and unlike most humans in the current epoch, they allowed their souls to shine brightly for all to see. They were the most authentic and loving creatures I had ever encountered.

But from the time I first saw him fleeing the back porch light, there was something about Slow Loris that represented all the best this world can muster. He was the most suspicious and the most vulnerable at the same time. His skittish way around other humans was only surpassed by the affection he showered on his brothers and upon us. I told him he was my new role model. And I meant it. To this day he crawls up on our pillows every night and sleeps right beside our heads, purring us to sleep with gratitude and contentment.

I knew after a very short time that this was a very special creature, whose spirit had seen many things in lives already past. I also began to see how he was being constantly targeted for destruction by evil forces and that it would be my job to protect this little White Buffalo Calf from these forces of darkness that attempt to rule this world through the royal bloodline.

It took him two days to wake up from the anesthesia the veterinarian had given him when he got neutered. The vet later told me he had to give him an extra shot because he was so strong-willed.

Once, he was bitten by a copperhead and his foot swelled up to the size of an orange. We fed him endless amounts of peach yogurt and he got better. Another time while I was gone for a week campaigning for Bernie Sanders in Des Moines, Iowa, he tore a ligament jumping from a tree. We kept him in the house and massaged his leg and he eventually healed up.

Then one night at 3:00 AM I heard a blood-curdling cry in the yard. I ran out completely naked, knowing it was one of the boys. Slow Loris was being attacked from the air and I scared the attacker away. Loris was limping but alive. As I scooped him up to bring him inside, my mind said it was a great horned owl. But my soul said it was some alien force. And the more I learned about owls, it was probably both since the weirdos use owls as messengers. They sometimes use skunks as well. This is because the Crown and its secret societies operate under the cover of darkness and these are nocturnal animals. Indians will tell you that if you see an owl close by you should be on guard because something bad is about to happen. It's not the owl's fault. They are just the messenger.

After all the attacks on Slow Loris we were shocked when in early 2017 it was Harvey Wall Banger and Silent Bob who tragically died within five weeks of each other. Harvey was run over by a greasy hippie wannabe who should never have come to our house. I blamed myself. Bob succumbed to heartworm. He was the most independent of the bunch and had spent too many nights outside. Again, I blamed myself.

We were devastated. Death seemed to hang over the place and we decided it was time to go. Slow Loris was sad, too, and seemed to agree. So we put our 40-acre farm up for sale. Two years later we finally sold it and on a whim, we headed northwest for a new stronghold. After all his scrapes, it was Slow Loris who had survived to make the journey across the flat lands to the Black Hills of western South Dakota.

Much of the injustice and suffering in this world occurs due to haste. When people are in a hurry, they are captive to their "rational" mind – a construct created by the Crown to enslave humanity. The natural way to live involves living in the now and paying close attention to our surroundings. With the increase in screen time in recent years, the whole world seems to have attention deficit disorder. This lack of attentiveness has created a collective ignorance in the population, which is then celebrated by the Crown's corporate media as "cool".

But Slow Loris will have none of it. He is governed by only two rules: love and attentiveness to his pride (which is now just Jill and I) and to the natural world both of which are coupled with a great and very healthy skepticism of the intentions of all other humans. And whenever I get in a hurry, I look at Slow Loris and remember the profound message delivered to me by Crazy Horse.

Chapter 3

Wakan Tanka & The Good Red Road

Wakan Tanka is a Lakota word that best translates as "the great mystery". For Crazy Horse and his fellow Lakota people, Wakan Tanka is God. Not some white male with a long beard who lives in the sky, as the Crown religions would have us believe. Not one of many gods in a pagan pantheon as misinformed Crown-inspired liberals would have us believe. No, Wakan Tanka is the monotheistic Creator of all.

The humility expressed in this understanding of the nature of reality can only be appreciated when one compares it to the two supposedly opposing views of the dominant culture. One arm of this Crown-informed worldview tells us that "science" rules all and that there is no God. These fools tell us that everything in the universe came from a "big bang", which though still an unproven theory is paraded around as "science".

These humans apparently cannot see the meticulous way in which this world was put together, with different plants providing food for different animals, different weather occurring throughout the year to nourish those plants, different coastal tides, and upper-level winds creating that weather, and so on.

Lakota elders will tell you that Wakan Tanka made it all this way. Genesis 6 will tell you pretty much the same thing. But this second arm of the Royal Society-informed worldview likes to ignore this and many other parts of a certain history book known as the bible. Their mission in life is to save the souls of heathens like the Lakota people whose "original sin" was ostensibly that they clearly understood the nature of reality.

The Lakota know that humans did not come from the sky, they came from the earth. They know that "heaven" is not in the sky where the Anunnaki came from, but here on earth, if we simply accept and show humility and gratitude towards Wakan Tanka's beautiful and perfect creation. They know there is no original sin to overcome since this regards the story of Adam & Eve, who rejected this understanding of the nature of reality in favor of lies told to them by an Anunnaki serpent related to King Sargon. Central to this lie was eating forbidden fruit from the tree of knowledge, which is a metaphor for human beings worshiping their intellect rather than having faith in a higher-power that is more connected to our heart and soul, but most importantly, to our natural animal instincts.

For this reason, the Lakota and other indigenous people do not naturally wrestle with such concepts as guilt and shame. And who, when left to their own devices, never left their Garden of Eden for over 100,000 years of relative peace. They survived and thrived from the bounty of nature through a blend of deep love for their family and clan and great suspicion towards outsiders. They did not adopt the preconceived notions that the royal bloodline came to call "science" and "religion". Instead, they were true scientists who observed, inferred, and made educated guesses as they made their way through life. They were much more in tune with the laws of nature than any religion has been henceforth.

What we Crown-educated dualists came to call science and religion, would simply be called the Good Red Road by them. This is not a "belief", but an intuitive understanding of the nature of reality in which reciprocity is necessary to have a good life, since giving is nature's supreme law. If one takes too much, one will suffer the consequences. If one over-hunts the bison, the herd disappears. If one over-fishes the trout stream, it will go barren. If one plants too many times in a certain place, the nutrients will be depleted from the soil and crops will no longer grow there.

It's not that indigenous people were overly spiritual beings, as many on the fake left would have you believe. Those notions of "spirituality", including paganism, were invented by the royal bloodline in Babylon as a means to deceive people. In fact, the royals consider themselves pagans. Druids to be exact. It's just that Indians were real scientists and came to understand that in order to thrive they must do things a certain way and reciprocate whenever possible with their natural relatives to receive the bounty provided by Wakan Tanka.

Central to this understanding is that all living things are related. How can I radio-collar a bear then track and monitor the bear to "protect" it if I have a relationship with that bear and know that wearing the collar will make it angry? Maybe this lack of humility regarding the value of bears will even lead that bear to attack and eat humans.

The Lakota thanked the tatanka (bison) every time they finished hunting them. They considered the bison to be better than they were since they gave their very lives to keep the tribe from going hungry. Of course, they were forced to rely more heavily on bison only after the wetiko settlers and their army protectors showed up, forcing the Lakota to abandon their crops and become even more nomadic than the semi-nomads they originally were just to get away from them

Indians will always tell you how important it is to have a relationship with the animals they hunt since this relationship is necessary if the animals are to give themselves up to the hunter. Yet this reality is denied by the dominant culture, which is inculcated with the absurd idea that animals cannot communicate with each other and we cannot talk to them, either.

And where does this illogical idea come from? From the Crown of course. But this time, it's the courtesy of their Royal Geographic Society tentacle, the same one that insists that humans evolved from apes and hinges that assumption on evolutionary theory. This theory, paraded again as solid "science", has a small problem. There has never been a solid genetic link established between apes and men. For years, they marched out *Ramapithecus*, until it, too, was shot down by real science.

Walking the Good Red Road must, by its very nature, be done slowly and with great attention to both detail, and to occurrences in the natural world. What the Western world has done instead is to block out and ignore nature, while operating on "scientific" preconceptions they learned from the Crown and its numerous official tentacles.

In doing so, Western man denies the very nature of reality. For example, in traditional Lakota culture, the man who kills the hunted animal not only thanks his relative for giving its life, but he also eats last when the meat is cooked for the tribe to eat. This is not because the man is "woke". This man was never asleep in the first place.

He does so because he understands the nature of reality in which action always produces a reaction, where instant karma is a given. He knows that by eating last he will earn or retain deep respect from other members of the tribe. And that respect will make his life much easier going forward. He knew what my three cats knew. It is not, therefore, as the dualistic Crown "experts" would have you believe, a selfless act, but rather a very selfish act. He is looking out for his best interests and in doing so the best interests of the tribe are also served. This is how the world actually works.

When a person truly looks out for his or her self, they help the greater good, since the universe is not based on a law where one must sacrifice to do good. Rather, doing the right thing brings bounty to the actor. They are one and the same. Conversely, when people do the wrong thing, it always and without exception brings them pain and suffering, which then reverberates out into the greater world.

The Lakota understood this as the Sacred Hoop. The nature of reality was not laid out in straight lines. It was circular. Any action would eventually work its way around that circle and back to the actor. But it wasn't just the Lakota who understood this. Every tribe on planet earth accepted this as scientific fact, with over 100,000 years of experience to back it up.

This truism is reflected in the legend of the Ouroboros, where the snake or dragon, due to the circular nature of reality, will eventually, after devouring all else, eat its own tail. And that is exactly what is going on today as the Crown devours all the resources of the planet, eventually consuming even themselves as the circular action completes.

There is no duality, only polarity. It's all about energy, electricity, and sending out good vibes which then resonate throughout all creation. Feeling good about and loving yourself is where it all begins. Seeing ourselves in a relationship with the rest of the world, rather than in competition with it, is the key. There is nothing natural about capitalism.

For this reason, indigenous cultures did not have kings or queens, or even chiefs. The tribal "chief" was a Crown fabrication that made it easier for the colonizers to control the tribes and steal their land and resources. Typically, government officials beholden to the Crown would pick individuals within the tribes who were weak and easily corrupted to become "tribal chiefs". They could then bribe these stooges, sometimes with something as simple as a bottle of whiskey. Countless bad treaties were signed by "tribes" throughout the world in this manner. And this practice continues to this day in our political arena.

Instead, tribes were governed very loosely and by a council of mainly elderly members, both men and women. Inequality between the sexes began with the advent of agriculture, a subject I will delve into further later in this book. It also became more exaggerated with the rise of capitalism, which we will also explore in later chapters.

One could argue that the Indians were anarchists. In other words, they rejected all forms of "archy", which means some people "arch over" or control others. Patriarchy, matriarchy, oligarchy, and monarchy are all Crown concepts that reinforce rule by bloodline – or the "divine right of kings" concept. But these relationships do not exist in nature. They exist only in the demented minds of the perpetrators of colonial theft and violence.

The concept of the alpha male is also a phony contrived concept based on a fear and misunderstanding of the nature of reality. Translated correctly from Greek, alpha means "pure". It has nothing at all to do with physical size or strength, the size of one's bank account, or the power one wields over a society. In fact, one could argue that in the latter two cases such a person is the opposite of alpha – a weak and cowardly individual who resorted to some form of exploitation or cheating to attain that status. Nothing pure about that.

The recent Covid-19 psyop illustrates how insane the Crown methodology, or lack thereof, is. Here, one must be reminded that coronavirus translates to English as "crown venom". Although no one on this planet has yet isolated a virus of any kind, germ "theory" is again paraded around as fact by Crown tentacles such as the Lancet Journal and the *New England Journal of Medicine*.

Meanwhile, few "scientists" observed that the arrival of crown venom directly coincided with a massive build-out of wireless communications infrastructure, culminating in the 5G network. Although many studies have been conducted regarding the negative health effects of electromagnetic frequencies to both humans and the non-human world, those who cite those studies (including at least one by the US Navy) are disregarded as "conspiracy theorists". In fact, we have entered a time when any idea that calls into question the centuries-old lies of the Crown is a "conspiracy theory".

Indigenous people have words for this type of insanity that replaces their solid understanding of a reality based on love with a hurried panic-stricken mentality based on fear. To the Indians, this insanity devours not just flesh, like a cannibal would, but devours souls, as well.

The Cree call it *wetiko*. The Algonquin call it *wendigo*. And as you can tell from Crazy Horse's name translated, the Lakota call it *witko*. These tribes did not encounter the carriers of this mind virus until around 1850 or so. This explains why their creation stories make the most sense. They were not corrupted by the lies of the royal bloodline until very recently. The history book known as the bible does not even pertain to them. They knew nothing of the East India Company, capitalism or industrialism until 170 years ago.

This wetiko insanity emanates from the royal bloodline. They do not originate from this earth so the laws of nature are foreign to them. This mindset is synonymous with the Archons of ancient Gnostic writings, the Nephilim fallen angels of the bible, the

Anunnaki invaders identified by the Sumerian clay tablets and the *jinn* of ancient Islamic teachings. It is also synonymous with artificial intelligence, aliens, Lucifer, Satan, the devil, and virtual reality.

Lakota mythology does not have a concept of pure evil because they were insulated from the crimes of the royal Nephilim bloodline for centuries. They could never have imagined such insane ideas or behavior from creatures who appear to be human. Thus the word wetiko to describe them.

In fact, evil is not native to this world. Wakan Tanka made it perfect. But evil had happened before on our planet when alien invaders made their way here and lived out their twisted wetiko ways. For example, we are told in the Book of Enoch, which is conveniently left out of most bibles, that giants once roamed the earth. And new scientists are now unearthing their massive, elongated skulls to prove it.

Enoch, who was Noah's grandfather, said God came to him and told him to tell the giants to quit eating human flesh or they would be vanquished from the earth. They did not listen and soon Noah was busy building an arc in preparation for God's unhappy response to the giants' behavior. These giants were somehow related to the same Nephilim bloodline that currently rules this world via parasitic capitalism. The appearance is more refined, but in a very real sense they are again "eating" people.

Wakan Tanka had answered these interventions of evil at various earlier times. Along with the Great Flood, we also know of an Ice Age that wiped out a huge chunk of the earth's population. There was also the Lake Toba, Sumatra, supervolcano, then later, a giant meteor strike in the Yucatan Peninsula, to name just a few of God's answers to evil past.

The most recent intervention like this occurred in Sumeria approximately 8,500 years ago. Evil had arrived on this earth again and for the first time a ruling clique declared itself a "royal bloodline". People would again be tested as to their understanding of he nature of reality. The question was the same as it had always been. Would we remember?

Chapter 4

The Anunnaki Bloodline: From Sumeria to Egypt

With the help of an army of ancient historians, archaeologists, anthropologists, physicists, astronomers, and linguists a "new science" has emerged in the past few decades. This development – part of the great remembering – has rattled the Crown's "scientific" institutions, which have counted on obfuscation and inversion of what they know as the seven sacred sciences of the Nephilim to keep humanity in the dark regarding our true nature and the nature of reality.

These seven are rhetoric, logic, grammar, arithmetic, geometry, music, and astronomy. While these are indeed important sciences, the key to the Crown's control over the human mind is to corrupt these seven disciplines to deceive people. They call this inversion of science "black magic". Put more simply these are lies.

A major breakthrough for the new people's science came when archaeologists working in modern-day Iraq unearthed a large number of clay tablets from the muddy estuary between the Tigris and Euphrates Rivers near Basra in what is now Iraq. Scribbled on the tablets was a strange cuneiform language, written by the inhabitants of what was then known as Sumeria. These writings remain the oldest known to modern man.

A few scholars were able to translate these writings into English. The most famous of these was Azerbaijan native Zecharia Sitchin, who learned to translate Sumerian cuneiform while working as a shipping clerk in Bak, Azerbaijan. Sitchin later graduated from the London School of Economics and wrote many books on his findings before his death in 2010.

Like his predecessors, Immanuel Velikovsky and Eric von Daniken, Sitchin's translations of the Sumerian clay tablets led him to the conclusion that an extra-terrestrial race of beings had landed in the Middle East region nearly 8,500 years ago, leading to many major changes for the human population on this planet.

In his many books, including *The 12th Planet* and *Lost Book of Enki*, Sitchin writes at length as to what these tablets actually say. They talk of beings they called the Anunnaki, who arrived in Sumeria after their planet, Nibiru, collided with another planet and lost its protective ozone layer. The Anunnaki came here to mine gold with which to concoct a gold-based flecking that would be used to reconstruct their ozone layer. It turns out that NASA recently used this same kind of gold flecking to patch up our ozone layer.

The two Anunnaki commanders of this mission were named Enki and Enlil. Another was named Nazi. They instructed the Sumerian humans that they called *adamus*, to *avod* (work for) or worship them since they were "gods". They conducted experiments on the humans out of which were bred a new slave race to mine their gold beneath the soil of modern-day South Africa. They also bred a new class of rulers by mixing Anunnaki and human DNA to produce a new royal bloodline.

The tablets also talk about how humans were forced from their long-practiced hunting and gathering existence into a new way of living that we now call agriculture. This is a collective human decision that has baffled serious cultural anthropologists for decades. Why did tribal semi-nomadic people move from the much easier hunting and gathering life to one involving the hard work that is agriculture?

The Sumerian clay tablets say these Mesopotamians were forced into it by Anunnaki space invaders. This area has always been regarded as the place where farming began. Now we may have our answer as to why. Soon, the ancient cities of Babylon, Akkad, Uruk, Kish, and Ur were formed under hybrid bloodline rule and the human agriculturalists were forced to supply these Anunnaki-controlled cities with food.

Less than 4,600 years ago, in 2334 BC, King Sargon, a representative of these Anunnaki/human hybrids and their self-proclaimed royal bloodline, became the first king the world had ever known. He conquered all of southern Mesopotamia, as well as parts of what are now Iran, Syria, and Turkey. Interestingly, King Sargon spoke the Semitic language of Akkadian and not Sumerian. The rise of the Semitic languages in west Asia and northern Africa has always been tricky for mainstream science to explain but it coincided with the Anunnaki intervention.

The word Semitic has nothing to do with the Jewish religion. It is simply used to describe a group of people in a certain region who speak this category of languages. So by definition, if one is accused of being anti-Semitic, a tactic often used by the ruling elite to silence critics of their global oligarchy, one is actually being accused, not of being anti-Jewish, but of being in opposition to the royal Anunnaki bloodline.

A similar etymological game is played with the word Zionism. Again Zionism has nothing to do with Jews. Zion is a transliteration of the word *scion*, which means to graft. In this case, the project is to graft the Anunnaki bloodline with the human race in order to corrupt and control us. Initial Anunnaki DNA experiments likely occurred near Mt. Zion in modern-day Israel, giving it that name. Both the Tribe of Dan and the Canaanites were corrupted people who lived at the base of Mt. Zion. So again, if one is an anti-Zionist, it does not mean they hate the Jewish religion. It means they are opposed to the Nephilim's grafting of their "fallen angel" bloodline onto human DNA.

While Mesopotamia is well-known as the place where agriculture was born, King Sargon also established commercial ties to the Indus Valley, which is known as another very early center of agriculture.

With the advent of agriculture came the rise of a new class system, since if one farmer's crop failed he may be at the mercy of another farmer for food. Farming was done not by tribes of people, but by extended families who were closely related by blood. Bloodlines were suddenly becoming central to how humans operated, supplanting a broader understanding that we were all related and should work together rather than, in this case, compete for the biggest crop yield against other bloodline family units.

It was at this point that humans began to forget that the entirety of life on this planet is a relative and should be treated as such. With the rise of agriculture came a new human paranoia towards nature, since a farmer's crops could be devastated by hail, while his newly domesticated cattle could fall prey to wolves. Each family would protect its own farm, so a certain level of mistrust developed between even neighboring farmers.

A successful farmer would soon become the area banker as he could borrow grain to others at interest. A human reality that had been based for hundreds of thousands of years on equality and reciprocity was quickly being replaced with one based on competition and a race to accumulate the most material possessions for their new sedentary life.

The concept of land ownership was born as formerly semi-nomadic peoples became sedentary sharecroppers on land seized by the Anunnaki Crown. With the rise of cities and their necessary sewage disposal and water systems came the rise of water-borne diseases. Nature had not meant for people to live in such large concentrations. Now, many would die as disease spread quickly because of unsanitary conditions.

Around this same time, sprawling temples built skyward towards the "gods" began to appear simultaneously around the world – from Angkor Wat in Cambodia to Machu Picchu in Peru, from the pyramids of Giza in Egypt to Tikal in Guatemala. To this day historians struggle to explain how these wonders of the world were built, who built them, and why. Certainly, there must have been a "high-technology" component to the construction of these megaliths.

The Anunnaki hybrids began to expand geographically, with King Sargon and his proteges seizing territory in every direction. In addition to the Tribe of Dan and the Canaanites, hybrid clans also included the Hittites, the Akkadians, the Kassites, and the Babylonians.

In Babylon, the hybrid "gods" taught humans new concepts they called "religion" and "spirituality", while they dabbled in dark arts based on deception and secrecy. The legend of the Tower of Babel states that before the tower was built all humans in the world spoke the same language. Some scholars believe the tower is the Etemenanki ziggurat, which was erected in Babylon at the behest of Marduk, a prominent Anunnaki royal. Other researchers say it was King Nimrod of Shinar who authorized the construction of the Tower of Babel. The bible tells us that Nimrod was the son of Cush, making him a great-grandson of Noah.

The legend goes that once the tower was built Yahweh punished the people by scrambling the world's languages so that no tribe could understand the language of the other. Many scholars also believe that Yahweh himself was an Anunnaki patriarch. It is interesting that many Native American traditions also talk of a time when their languages were scrambled so tribes could not communicate with one another. Some tribes claim that animals also shared this common language with humans so that they could communicate easily with us.

It makes sense. If you are attempting to colonize and conquer a new planet, the last thing you would want is for people to start talking about it, lest they form a resistance to it. The advent of computers, cell phones, and the internet has had the very same effect on people in the modern world. We hardly talk to each other anymore. Instead, we isolate ourselves further in an Orwellian virtual hell called "social media". Talk about inversion.

The practice of ritual sacrifice of both humans and animals also spread like wildfire out of Babylon and around the world, especially in places where the aforementioned "sky god" temples were built. Peaceful tribes like the Aztecs of central Mexico were suddenly famous for their bloodthirsty sacrifices. Mainstream archaeologists have tried to explain this away in various Crown-funded directions.

Many have used it to convince people that indigenous people were inherently brutish and violent – a lie that the historical record simply does not support. Some posit that the tribes became overpopulated or that a drought caused them to begin sacrificing people. This doesn't make sense either. Overpopulation was never a problem for indigenous people since hunting and gathering was a simple, but dangerous life. And drought could always be avoided by simply relocating, a constant practice for semi-nomads.

I am convinced that these tribes began performing sacrifices because they were threatened and corrupted by the Anunnaki builders of the "sky god" temples to do so. Indigenous cultures did not believe they came from the sky. Their cosmology reflects a consistent belief that they quite literally came out of the earth. So why would they even build such ostentatious structures? Were they also forced into agriculture, like the Sumerians, to feed the new royal occupants of these temples and their new regional cities?

Back in Babylon, a group of Radhanite bankers emerged, led by the Marushu and Agibi families. They introduced the idea of usury on this planet, while controlling all facets of life in Babylon. They also introduced Talmudic Judaism as the religion of Babylon. The Talmud mocks Jesus and encourages pedophilia among its followers.

The Grand Lodge of Cairo became another hybrid power center after Marduk, Enki, and Enlil took over Egypt. Here they were called pharaohs rather than kings. The first Egyptian pharaoh was Narmer in 3150 BC, although members of the Anunnaki royal bloodline dynasty were not officially recognized as pharaohs until around 1200 BC. It is hard not to notice the elongated skulls of pharaohs such as King Tut.

The Anunnaki knew this area well, as many scholars believe they initially landed their spacecraft on Egypt's Sinai Peninsula. Out of the pharaoh-funded Grand Lodge of Cairo emerged the Brotherhood of the Snake, the first known royal bloodline-controlled secret society that eventually morphed into Freemasonry, the

Muslim Brotherhood, and the Kabbalah, depending on the religious cover of the adept.

These secret societies carried out various dirty tasks for the royal Anunnaki bloodline using a veneer of respectability to hide their heinous acts. They operate in the same manner to this day, concealing the Crown's human, drugs and arms trafficking operations behind an array of parades, circuses and charitable children's hospitals.

While many of the Anunnaki bloodline became the Egyptian pharaohs, another branch headed north to the Caucasus Mountains between the Black Sea and the Caspian Sea from what is now Sochi, Russia, to Baku, Azerbaijan. These Khazarian people called themselves Ashkenazi Jews, though they were actually Anunnaki pagans. They took over trade routes into Asia, especially the ancient Silk Road and introduced Yiddish as the secret language of the Silk Road trade, which involved much slavery and human trafficking.

However, these "Ashkenazi Jews" were actually the Babylonian Radhanite bankers who had usurped the name from Noah's great-grandson, Ashkenon, as a religious cover for their Talmudic usury and to gain sympathy in their battle with Turkish and Mongol forces along this highly-strategic trade route.

One of these Khazarian families was the Baccarats, who later became the Bauer family, and who are currently known as the Rothschilds. The Baccarats later teamed up with the Venetian banking families to lend money for the formation of the Hanseatic League. They also lent money to the various bloodline monarchs across Europe. They would become widely known as "court Jews" or *Hofjuden*.

Disguised as Jews, these Radhanite Frankish pagans could charge interest to their clients. After the Protestant Reformation and an easing of usury laws, some of these families converted to Christianity. Meanwhile, some of the court Jews, such as the Rothschilds, intermarried with the bloodline and became royalty themselves.

Back in Egypt, the Anunnaki pharaohs busied themselves enslaving the local populations to build pyramids that, to this day, symbolize their operational plan to enslave humanity. The pyramids built at Giza, using slave labor and some sort of anti-gravity technology, are a reminder to earth's human population of the top-down command structure of the royal bloodline. A few at the top control the masses at the bottom. For each level up the pyramid one goes, the corruption, nepotism, and material wealth grows greater.

This is why the United States Federal Reserve, which is largely owned by eight families: Rockefeller, Rothschild, Kuhn Loeb, Goldman Sachs, Warburg, Lehman/Oppenheimer, Israel Moses Seif, and Lazard, adopted the pyramid symbolism used on its US $1 note. The Fed is a private banking cartel, not a government agency, as laid out in my 2014 book, *The Federal Reserve Cartel*.

Much of this symbolism can also be found in Freemasonry. In Scottish Rite Freemasonry, by far the most powerful branch, with York Rite being the other, there are 33 levels. This symbolizes the human backbone, which contains 33 vertebrae. Once a Freemason attains the 33rd degree, he is then eligible to become a member of the Illuminati. This will only happen if he is, by this time, very corrupt and willing to take part in heinous and sadistic rituals.

The Illuminati represents the head or brain of the human body. Members consider themselves more enlightened or illuminated than other humans, so they take it upon themselves to serve as the brains of the human race. The most powerful bankers, business leaders, military commanders, and politicians along with media, technology and defense executives are members of this "brain trust".

Atop the Illuminati head sits the Crown, which does not even have to think. They simply live a life of leisure like any true owner of the planet would do, occasionally showing up in public to perform some meaningless but highly symbolic task, to remind us who is really in charge. I'll get into the royal bloodline command structure in more detail later in this book.

The Israelites who were enslaved by the pharaohs to help build their pyramids were not the same people who inhabit Israel today. They were black tribal people, many of whose ancestors now reside in Ethiopia and other parts of north Africa. Jesus himself, who railed against the Anunnaki-introduced blood sacrifices in the temples of

Jerusalem as well as against their practices of slavery and usury, was almost certainly a black man.

In 1945, a major discovery was unearthed near the north Egyptian town of Nag Hammadi. Thirteen leather-bound books were dug up by a local farmer. Written by Gnostics, the 52 treatises contained in the books became known as the Nag Hammadi Scrolls or The Gnostic Gospels.

Written in the Coptic language, the books contain the full Gospel of Thomas along with the writings of several other of Jesus' apostles and some of the gospels of Jesus himself. They are currently housed at the Coptic Museum in Cairo. Two years later the Dead Sea Scrolls were discovered at Qumran in Palestine.

Both scrolls discuss an intervention upon the earth by aliens and the Nag Hammadi Scrolls describe evil entities that the Gnostics referred to as Archons. Notice the root word "arch" again.

The Archons are described as "alien false king tyranny rulers" who controlled people through masks of deception. They ruled through "war and the use of high technology, including mind control and frequency implants". The scrolls indicate that the perpetrators were both human and non-human but that the command structure was located in the Orion Constellation – where many researchers believe the Reptilian and Draconian alien races call home.

The Gnostics claim to have encountered these inorganic beings who feed off human psychic energy and see our planet as a resource for them to consume. Ronald Bernhard, a Dutch businessman turned Illuminati whistleblower, has talked about how the Freemason project in this world is to literally turn humans into batteries, ostensibly to power their royal Anunnaki bloodline controllers and their off-planet kin.

The last of the Egyptian pharaohs was Cleopatra VII, who was born in 69 BC. It was no coincidence that the Egyptian empire, then on the verge of bankruptcy, was about to collapse just as the Roman Empire was being born.

In fact, Cleopatra VII, the only Egyptian pharaoh who ever bothered to learn the Egyptian language, became a lover of Roman General Julius Caesar just as a revolution against the pharaohs began to rumble through the streets of Cairo. Huddled behind palace walls in the city, she gave birth to a son named Caesarion (son of Caesar), then fled across the Mediterranean to Rome as the revolutionaries closed in, only to return to Egypt after Caesar was assassinated in 44 BC.

It was also no coincidence that the Library at Alexandria, considered the most comprehensive source for ancient history scholars of the time, was burned to the ground as the Egyptian pharaohs gave way to the Roman emperors. Most scholars believe it was Julius Caesar himself who was responsible for having the library destroyed.

It makes sense. If you were part of a secret extraterrestrial royal bloodline that was about to move its power center from the Middle East across the Mediterranean Sea and into southern Europe, you would want to destroy all evidence that you were the very same bloodline that landed and ruled Sumeria and Babylon before conquering Egypt.

Chapter 5

The Unholy Roman Empire

Historians on the Crown payroll would have us believe that there is absolutely no connection between the Egyptian pharaohs and their Sumerian Anunnaki predecessors. They would also have us believe that the decline of Egypt and the rise of the Holy Roman Empire were completely coincidental. As you've just read, this is simply not true.

Cleopatra consummated the furtherance of royal bloodline control over the planet through her eugenics-driven affair with Julius Caesar just as the bloodline was being forced by Egyptian revolutionaries to relocate to a new zip code.

But you won't hear this from any "Egyptologist", whose funding depends on the glorification of these supposedly omnipotent "gods". One has to ask why such a field of study even exists. By now you probably know the answer. It's the same reason we are inculcated with Italophile and Anglophile views. The peasants must revere both past and present power centers of the royal Anunnaki bloodline.

The truth is that over last 8,500 years, the Babylonian empire never actually died. Neither did the Roman or British Empires. They are the same bloodline empire that has simply changed its base of operations, partly due to more strategic geography, partly to keep researchers of geopolitical power at bay, and partly because the local populations over which they rule get tired of the wetiko ways of these cosmic carpetbaggers and tend to rise up against them.

The Holy Roman Empire is officially said to have lasted from 962 AD to 1806 AD. But the reality is that it began just as the pharaohs were being run out of Egypt during the time of Jesus' birth. It was Jesus' refusal to pledge allegiance to the ever-expanding Roman empire of Caesar and his criticism of the corrupt Jewish stooges of the Romans in Jerusalem, like Pontius Pilate, that ultimately cost him his life. Jesus was fighting the Crown and he was killed by the Crown. It's that simple.

The Roman Empire did not take on the prefix "Holy" until it had thoroughly taken over the Roman Catholic church. The emperors were pagans, just like their Anunnaki ancestors. But they needed a religion to hide behind and Jesus' popularity made the Catholic religion the best choice. They had also learned that they could use religion as a political battering ram, passing edicts easily by convincing the serfs that they were God's representatives on this earth and were carrying forward policies that God sanctioned, no matter how brutal.

Jesus had hand-picked his disciple, Peter, as the rock on which his new Christian church would be built. Initially, Peter set out for Turkey where he founded his first church at Antioch, now Antakya. At the time, it was part of Constantinople in the Eastern Roman Empire. Some of his flock looked east and became Eastern Orthodox Christians. Others looked west and became Roman Catholics.

In 325 AD, the royal bloodline Roman Emperor Constantine I called the First Council of Nicaea. It was here that the bloodline began the corruption of Jesus' church. They called for Jesus' brutal death to be celebrated as Easter. Prior to this, Easter had been a time of mourning. To the bloodline, this was simply another blood sacrifice.

Jesus was declared by the council to be the only son of God and elevated to messiah status, something that Jesus himself had warned his disciples against doing. Most Christians at this time understood that Jesus was no more divine than any of the rest of us should strive to be, because that's what he taught them. These Christian sects, including Jesus' own Essenes, along with the Gnostics and the Cathars, from which the Catholic Church took its name, were deemed heretics by the First Council of Nicaea.

The council also enshrined canon law, which allowed the Catholic hierarchy to issue papal bulls and dictates without the consent of the church rank and file. This was essentially the first legal system in the modern world. But of course, there was no due process and no recourse for the damned.

Once the fix was in and Christian beliefs were corrupted, one by one a succession of Roman emperors and their stooges in various parts of the Roman Empire began to publicly convert from paganism to Catholicism. Privately, they loathed Jesus as a wild-eyed revolutionary and remained as pagan as any pure-blood Anunnaki invader.

With canon law in place, the Roman Empire could now use religion as a justification for the bloody colonial expansion the royal bloodline was about to undertake. By concealing their true intentions behind a veneer of righteousness, they hoped to fool the indigenous hunters and gatherers that they were about to rape, pillage, and exterminate all around the world. They had learned their lesson in Egypt and going forward, they would have to show at least a modicum of humanity to subdue their potential subjects.

Legend has it that Babylonian bloodline King, Nebuchadnezzar II, destroyed King Solomon's Temple in Mount Moriah, Israel, in 576 BC. However, many scholars now question whether the temple ever existed in the first place. Whatever the case may be, in 1119, a group calling itself the Order of Solomon's Temple moved its headquarters to the site of the fabled temple.

They claimed allegiance to the recently consecrated Holy Roman Empire, but more specifically, to the Pope. Their official purpose was to protect Christian pilgrims from Europe traveling to the Middle East to pay homage to the new "holy land". But their actual allegiance was to the Nephilim royal bloodline, which was now well-ensconced in Europe. Their real mission was to steal the assets of ordinary people and deliver the booty to the Crown.

In 1139, Pope Innocent II issued a papal bull known as *Omne datum optimum*, which translates as "every perfect gift". This gave "God's" approval to the actions of the Knights Templar. These actions included borrowing money to pilgrims who then paid them that same money back with interest in return for a guarantee of safe passage to the holy land.

Soon, the Templars were involved with all kinds of activities involving what we now call banking. In fact, the Templars can be seen as the founders of the very concept of banking. But they acted more like what we would call a mafia. They issued loans and collected those debts by whatever means necessary. They robbed any non-Christian they encountered and looted numerous valuable artifacts from the holy land, including the fabled Arc of the Covenant, which appears to have been some sort of high-technology free energy device. The Templars went to war with the Saracen Muslims in the Middle East and stole a large amount of gold which they began to store, along with their other ill-gotten wealth, at their Temple Mount headquarters.

It was no coincidence that the headquarters of the Templars was in a wing of the royal palace on the Temple Mount. After the Roman Army and the Franks had defeated the Fatimid Caliphate in 1099, they took over the Al-Aqsa Mosque and made it the home of King Baldwin II, instead. It is quite likely that, not only was the Temple Mount never built in ancient times, it was also never re-built because the royals actually stole the Al-Aqsa Mosque and became squatters.

This blows away the entire legend of Solomon's Temple, upon which the Knights Templar and their Freemason brethren rely on in order to amplify their self-importance to the rest of the world. Were they capable of building anything at all? They didn't need to. Better to let someone else build it and then kill the builders and take their property.

Whatever the case may be, King Solomon, King David, King Nebuchadnezzar, and King Baldwin II were all bloodline butchers who most certainly were not Christian in any way.

Throughout the various crusades, the Templars worked alongside the Knights Hospitaller and the Teutonic Knights to conquer the Middle East for the bloodline families that all three worked for. In 1229, during the 6th crusade, Holy Roman Emperor Frederick II reclaimed Jerusalem. But by 1244, the city was back in the hands of the Ayyubid dynasty, another royal bloodline. Much of their territory was then overrun by the Mongols under the command of yet another bloodline inbred named Genghis Khan.

The European-based bloodlines would not control Jerusalem again until they took it from the Ottoman Empire during WWI. And while the Order of the Knights Templar had officially lost the crusades, they had amassed a huge amount of wealth for the Holy Roman Emperor bloodline in the process. They had not only become the world's first bankers, but also the world's first multinational corporation.

Then, on Friday the 13th, October 1307, King Phillip IV of France, with the blessing of the new Pope, Clement V, ordered the arrest of Templar Grand Master Jacques de Molay and several other top ranking Knights Templar. American Freemasons honor de Molay to this day with their de Molay Society for children. The king and the pope tried to get the Templars and the Knights Hospitaller to merge, but neither wanted to do. It was also said that King Phillip owed the Templars a bunch of money.

The Templars were accused of numerous crimes including financial corruption, fraud, theft, worshiping idols (including Baphomet), and encouraging homosexuality, necromancy, and spitting on Jesus on the cross.

De Molay was burned at the stake and on November 22, 1307, Pope Clement issued Pastoralis Praeeminentiae, a papal bull instructing all Christian monarchs in Europe to seize the assets of the Order. This was followed by another bull that Pope Clement issued in 1312 at the Council of Vienne, which conveniently awarded most of the vast Templar wealth to the Knights Hospitaller, also known as the Knights of St. John of Jerusalem.

So while the Templars were officially disbanded on that now-famous and very unlucky Friday the 13th, the royal bloodline's mercenary/banker knights simply continued to carry out their skullduggery under a different name. Today, the Knights of St. John are headquartered in Valletta on the island of Malta. They are known as the Protestant faction of the royal guard, while the Catholic faction is known as the Knights of Malta.

In 1530, Pope Clement VII, who was himself a knight, struck a deal with Holy Roman Emperor Charles V who was also King of Spain and Sicily. This provided a permanent location for the Catholic knights on the island of Malta – right next to their Protestant Hospitaller brethren.

The 15th century brought significant advances in shipbuilding. From their base in Malta, both factions of Knights set out further afield to loot the parts of the world they hadn't already for the benefit of the Anunnaki Crown. The Knights Hospitaller occupied and controlled at least four Caribbean islands by 1600. Fabled explorers such as Columbus, Cortez, and Vespucci were all funded by the Crown.

Meanwhile, back in Europe, the royal bloodline that dispatched the knights had figured out that other islands and coastal cities could be used just like Malta to protect their wealth from the commoners who had no ships. Venice became a major banking center when, in 1587, the Republic of Venice launched its first public bank, Banco della Piazza di Rialto.

Many new science researchers have also identified the Bank of Venice, which they say was launched in the 12th century, making it the first bank in the world. This makes sense, because after the Templar rift with the Roman Catholic church, many of the Black Nobility fled to northern Italy, particularly Venice, and started banks with their ill-gotten gains. Genoa and Florence also became banking centers.

It is likely that the most powerful of these bloodline families were the Guistiniani clan. Another was the Bardi family, from which Queen Elizabeth II came. The di Medici, Lombard, Corsi, Cerchi, Massa, Candia, Foscari, Pallavicini, Fugger, and Welser families were also powerful Venetian bankers. All of these clans were related through the same royal bloodline.

Lest you think these families have faded into oblivion, as the Crown "scientists" would have you believe, they have not. Out of the Candias came the chocolate billionaire Mars family, and from the Welsers came the Wells family of Wells Fargo fame, as well as the Wellesley family. The Massas became the Massimo family. Obviously, it is common for these bloodline families to change their names slightly in order to throw off diligent researchers.

Today, Baron Girolamo de Massa is a powerful co-owner of Wells Fargo. Prince Hubertus Fugger-Babenhausen heads today's Fugger family. Alessandro Guistiniani has recently been both a senior economist at the International Monetary Fund and a Bank of Italy insider. Bank of America was formerly known as the Bank of Italy. The Pallavicinis' are related to both the British Cromwell family and the Shah of Iran. Alfonso Pallavicini was a top executive at BNP Paribas, which is now the largest bank in the world.

It was during these early days of Venetian banking that the concept of fascism developed. The idea was that these bloodline families would unite to protect each other's wealth under the threat of force. This immense private wealth would then merge with the state – in this case, the Holy Roman Empire – and the state would carry out policies that favored the bloodline families. Again, it is no coincidence that Mussolini's rise to power in Italy was funded by the Savoy family, who were the monarchy in Italy until it was "officially" dissolved.

Venice had its heyday, but it was another island that was destined to become even more powerful and central to the royal bloodline interests. They would call it, quite appropriately, the United Kingdom.

Chapter 6

The City of London

The Phoenicians knew a thing or two about shipbuilding, but between 1512 and 1915 the trade boomed and concentrated on the Thames River in and near the City of London. To this day, there is a livery company in the City of London known as the Worshipful Company of Shipwrights.

The Romans had already settled in this area in the 1st Century. Londinium, also called Roman London, was established in 47 AD. Viking invasions were frequent and the city was badly damaged. But in 886, the King of the Anglo-Saxons, Alfred the Great, renamed it Lundenburg, thus marking the launch of the City of London.

The Scandinavians also knew a thing or two about shipbuilding and inhabited a rugged and easily defensible coastline. In 1016, Cnut the Great took the City over for the Danish and Norwegian royals. For a time Cnut was king of all three fiefdoms, but by 1066, the Normans weighed in. Their invasion of England was led by the Duke of Normandy, who later became known as William the Conqueror.

Eventually, Norwegian King Harald's forces were defeated. From 1066 until his death in 1087, William was king of England. William descended from the royal Rollo bloodline. They were Vikings who had occupied Normandy for a time. Many other bloodline families had converged in Normandy, including the Hapsburg, Bourbon, Anjou, and Plantagenet dynasties, as well as the nearby northern Italian banking families. There was a period of interbreeding between these already closely related bloodlines prior to the Norman Invasion.

Interestingly this region, of what is now southern France and northern Spain, holds by far the world's majority of people with Rh-Negative blood. The other people who have this type are the royal bloodlines. And now these "blue bloods" would make the City of London their new global power center.

Also known as The Square Mile, the City of London is administered not by a democratic government, but by the City of London Corporation. Not officially part of either London or the United Kingdom the "City", as it is often referred to, is essentially a corporation. It sits next to Canary Wharf, which is London's central business district.

In 1215, King John of England signed Magna Carta Libertatum. Disguised as a charter of freedom, the Magna Carta was nullified, watered down, and then used by the Crown to extort taxes from their subjects. In the end, most of it was scrubbed from British statute books. But what the original document actually represented was a series of agreements between the Crown and the barons and the landed gentry of the region. It had nothing to do with expanding the rights of the people.

The Magna Carta was signed on Lombard Street, named for the Venetian Lombard banking family, in the City of London. It states clearly that "the City of London shall have/enjoy its ancient liberties".

In the same way the papal bulls had given the bloodlines moral cover, the Magna Carta codified ancient political and economic "liberties", making the City sovereign (just as monarchies are sovereign) from the interference or regulation of any government. Interestingly, there are no known records as to when the City of London Corporation was chartered.

The City is ruled by Freemen – an honor bestowed on certain unelected citizens. To become a City Alderman, one has to first be a Freemen. Freemason Lodges are omnipresent in the City, with most large banks having their own lodges. These banks also get to vote and the largest banks get the most votes. The City is ruled by a Lord Mayor who is the official head of the City of London Corporation. Until November 11, 2022, that was Vincent Keaveny, a member of the Knights Hospitaller, which is now known as the Order of St. John.

Just as in Cairo and Rome, the City and its Crown commanders experienced the occasional worker uprising against their hegemony. In 1381, rebels seized the City and occupied the Tower of London, which William the Conqueror had erected. Their leader, Wat Tyler, was killed in a battle that included Lord Mayor William Walworth. Again in 1450, rebel forces seized the City in what became known as the Jack Cade rebellion.

After falling out with the Catholic Church and bloodline migration towards northern Europe, much of the ill-gotten wealth of the Knights Templar ended up in Scotland. The Union of the Crowns in 1603 resulted in the official launch of the United Kingdom. The House of Plantagenet had become the House of Tudor. The rise of King James I ushered in the House of Stuart. They were all cousins, and with the Union of Crowns, they now ruled England, Scotland, Whales, and Ireland as the United Kingdom.

In 1689, King William III, a Protestant from the Dutch House of Orange/Nassau, took the UK throne after overthrowing his uncle and father-in-law, King James, in what became known as the Glorious Revolution. That same year, the Bill of Rights 1689 was passed by the UK Parliament.

By 1517, the Venetian bankers had successfully funded Martin Luther and Protestant Reformation. One of the key "reforms" was a new tenet that said a person's actions were not so important as long as they accepted Jesus as the messiah and only son God – taking the earlier Council of Nicaea mandates to a whole new level.

The bloodline bankers were amenable to this, knowing full well the rather odious nature of their long-practiced warfare, plundering, slavery, and usury. Though they maintained their Knights of Malta foothold in the Catholic Church, the royals would increasingly become Protestants. The Anglican Church, headquartered in the City of London, would become especially powerful. Also known as the

Church of England, it is affiliated with the Presbyterians in the United States and other parts of the world.

Once in power, King William III invited the Templars to bring their vast hidden Scottish booty into the City of London. It was after this huge wealth infusion that the City of London really took off as the global financial center. By the early 1700s, Scottish Rite Freemasonry, with help from the bloodline Sinclair (or St. Clair) family, was spreading like wildfire in the British Isles and beyond.

By 1691, Lombard Street was also home to Lloyd's Coffee House, which would soon become the world's biggest insurance market. In 1694, just three years later, the Bank of England was founded. In 1734, it moved its headquarters to Bank Junction on Threadneedle Street in the heart of the City of London. Some still refer to it as "The Old Lady of Threadneedle Street."

Barclays Bank had been in business as a goldsmith banker on Lombard Street since 1690. That same year, the oldest bank in the UK, C. Hoare & Co., which was founded in 1672, moved its headquarters to Fleet Street in the City of London. Two years later, Coutts & Co. bank was founded in the Strand.

Today, Coutts is a subsidiary of Natwest Holdings, which also owns the Royal Bank of Scotland (RBS) and Ulster Bank. Within four short years, the UK became home to three banking behemoths that still dominate global finance – Lloyds, Barclays, and RBS.

From the beginning, the Crown and the City were joined at the hip. Now under the Protestant King William III, began the coming out party for the royal Anunnaki bloodline, which had slithered its way from Sumeria to Babylon and Egypt, across the Mediterranean to Rome, up the coast to Venice, and finally to the British Isles. There was no more need for papal bulls or even religious pretense. Their fiefdoms were divided into new nations with the governments of those new nations beholden to their respective monarchies. These pretenses of law and democracy would now shield the bloodline from responsibility while at the same time doing its bidding in every arena.

In the city of London, the Temple Bar – whose name came from the Knights Templar – would come to signify the importance of

British Maritime Law or Crown Law in the forthcoming colonization and theft of resources around the world. This law prevails in the US today and is symbolized by gold fringe on US flags hung in every courtroom in the nation. US lawyers must pass a BAR exam before they begin practicing law. BAR stands for "British Accredited Regency".

Nearly a hundred years before the City gave birth to its global banking and insurance empire, the Crown had already figured out another way to shield it from responsibility – the multinational corporation. The City of London Corporation is no doubt the oldest corporation in the world. How old it is, we don't know for sure, because the papers seem to have been misplaced. However, many historians site the first such entity as the East India Company circa 1600.

Founded under a royal charter as The Governor and Company of Merchants of London Trading into the East Indies, it was a Crown Corporation with ties to the old Levant Company and before that, the Venice Company. Now it would be protected by the might of the growing British Empire. It was also the tip of the spear for the expansion of the British Empire. And with a "President's army" of 260,000 mostly Indian troops, it soon came to control vast swaths of land and resources in India and Southeast, and eventually, East Asia. By the mid-1700s, the East India Company controlled over half the global trade in commodities such as tea, cotton, indigo, spices, sugar, silk, salt, gunpowder, and opium.

The last two of these trade goods have remained staples of Crown revenue over the centuries. Mahatma Gandhi was once arrested at an anti-opium rally by East India Company puppets in Delhi. He was charged with, "disturbing the revenue".

The old Venetian bankers finally had their fascism. Going forward the royal bloodline would use state power rather than religious power to protect their financial interests in every corner of their new, but incredibly ancient British Empire. It was, again, no coincidence that Pax Britannica "officially" began in 1815, just nine years after the Holy Roman Empire officially came to an end in 1806.

Chapter 7

Farming Humanity

By the Middle Ages of the Holy Roman Empire, most of the people in Europe had become sharecroppers. As Mark Twain wrote in *A Connecticut Yankee in King Arthur's Court*, these serf subjects of the constantly-warring royal bloodline were compelled to give "half their crop to the Crown and a quarter of it to the Church", leaving very little for them to eat.

According to Zecharia Sitchin, the cuneiform writings on the Sumerian clay tablets tell of a local population of hunting and gathering tribes in the Mesopotamian region being forced into agriculture from their Garden of Eden existence by Anunnaki invaders from the planet Nibiru. They proclaimed to be gods and bred a human worker bee race to mine gold that would be used to patch up the ozone layer around their 12th Planet.

If the eerily similar temples built around the same time in all corners of the planet are any indication, the Anunnaki occupiers appear to have been quite the globetrotters. The pattern was similar. Invade an area, subjugate the foraging population into a difficult life of forced agriculture from which you feed, then put them to work as slaves in the building of your palatial temples which you then occupy as "gods" with a propensity for human sacrifice.

It was the beginning of the literal farming of humanity by the royal bloodline. And the beginning of the end of the understanding of the nature of reality for mankind.

Even as the Anunnaki hybrid royals were settling into Babylon and Ur, the new way of life for Sumerian farmers was taking its toll. Agriculture is hard work. It wears the body down quickly. It is also dangerous.

More importantly, it can be seen as a breaking point for human beings' relationships with their cousins in the natural world. These relationships informed people of the true nature of reality and produced a harmonious resonance that reverberated throughout creation.

If you wanted to bag a moose, you had better respect its family by protecting its habitat. If you wished to catch some salmon, you had better respect the river by keeping it clean. If you hoped to keep the peace with the bears, you should leave them some huckleberries and talk to them as you are picking near one another.

Farming turns this equitable and reciprocal reality upside down. Now there are crops to protect from coons, sheep to fence in from wolves, and chickens to guard from hawks. The natural world is quickly transformed from being a bountiful provider to being filled with dangerous and unpredictable enemies. Not the least of which is the weather.

Surely the bloodline knew this.

As a colonizing force, they were more than happy to break these ancient relationships that hunting and gathering cultures had with all aspects of the natural world. They knew that humans were strengthened by these bonds, which informed them of who they were. The colonizers wanted to weaken humans. Forcing them into either slave or sharecropper farming was a very effective means to do it. Soon agriculture sprang up simultaneously in many parts of the world.

King Sargon established commercial ties to the Indus Valley. In Mexico, crops first begin to appear between 8,000 and 9,000 years ago. China also traces its first agriculture to around 8,000 BC. So does South America. By 8,000 BC cattle had been domesticated as far west as the Iberian Peninsula. Pigs, sheep and, goats had been domesticated around 8,500 BC in Greece.

All of this coincides with the arrival of the Anunnaki royal invaders in Sumeria. Soon, oxen were bread to pull the plow and by 6,000 BC, horses had been domesticated in what is now Ukraine.

Humans were also being domesticated.

Slowly, their natural instincts were being shut down as they were forced into a sedentary existence. Ask any farmer today and they will tell you how their farm ties them down. I've experienced this firsthand, having farmed for the better part of forty years.

When a person doesn't move they become myopic and parochial. They no longer go to beautiful places for rest and celebration. They forget how beautiful those places are. They lose the electrical voltage that those places give them and the context they provide.

Tribes were slowly transformed into extended family clans. During the past century, we've seen the scattering of the extended family and the rise of single-family units. And in the past few decades, even these have been shattered into single-parent homes, further isolating people from one another and the nature of reality.

Gender inequality, which was nearly non-existent in hunting and gathering cultures, was by all accounts exacerbated by the rise of agriculture. Tribal councils nearly always included women. Most were elderly, like their male counterparts. There were no chiefs, only councils.

A never-before-seen class or caste system also developed alongside agriculture, as crop yields and weather varied and some farmers were forced to borrow grain from other farmers. Borrowing had never been much of an issue. Since tribal people didn't think of themselves as the "owners" of anything, how could anything be "borrowed"?

Now primarily sedentary, people began to accumulate material possessions. These new "owners" were increasingly anchored to their homestead because they were now "possessed". You see this today when people try to move and end up renting storage units that keep them anchored to a certain place.

Competition arose between farmers as to who could become the most "possessed". This is a competition that continues to this day. It was all madness to the natural world. The resonance was waning. And as Henry David Thoreau observed, "Material possessions are a positive hindrance to the elevation of mankind".

But the cruelest part of this forced transformation of human life was that the people in most cases weren't even allowed to own their own land, instead becoming sharecropper farmers on royal-owned land. Other workers of these bloodline fields were simply slaves.

By the 15th Century, the Kingdom of Castile had invaded the Canary Islands, where they subjugated the Guanches people to work as slaves in producing wine and sugar cane. They also traded these slaves with other royal estates along the Mediterranean.

By the 16th Century, with major advances in shipping, the transatlantic slave trade was in full swing. Funded by the monarchies of Portugal, Britain, Spain, and France, Africans were shipped across the Atlantic to work the Crown's newly "acquired" cotton, tobacco, cocoa, rice, coffee, and sugarcane plantations in North and South America.

The transatlantic slave trade persisted until US President Abraham Lincoln issued the Emancipation Proclamation in 1863, after over 12 million Africans had been abducted and sold into Crown slavery. An estimated 1.5 million died on slave ships on their way to the Americas. The largest share of these slaves were destined for Brazil and the Caribbean.

In the process, African tribes were torn asunder. Interestingly, the Africans resisted the global trend towards agriculture. Were they now being punished by the Anunnaki for their resistance to being farmed? It wasn't the first time the Africans had provoked the ire of the royal bloodline. And it wouldn't be the last.

Chapter 8

The East India Company: Slavery, Opium, and Adam Smith

At the epicenter of the transatlantic slave trade were the royal-chartered Dutch and British East India Companies. The Dutch East India Company was founded in 1602 by the House of Orange/Nassau, two years after the British version had been chartered by the Tudors. Also known as the United East India Company, it was the world's first joint-stock company and was especially active in the Spice Islands of what is now Indonesia.

There they busied themselves destroying hunting and gathering cultures while vacuuming up sharecropper and slave-farmed resources. Antwerp and Hamburg became major spice trading centers in Europe. There, the Dutch East India Company worked with the old Venetian Fugger and Welser families who now controlled this area, from which the Hanseatic League emerged.

According to company archives, the British East India Company shipped its first transatlantic slaves in 1684 from Madagascar to the British-controlled island of St. Helena in the South Atlantic. Meanwhile, they governed nearly the whole of India from their East India House headquarters on Leadenhall Street in the City of London. Demolished in 1862, just one year before Lincoln issued his Emancipation Proclamation, the site is now home to the Lloyd's building.

While European monarchs were funding expeditions to seize land and riches in the Americas, they were also funding the eradication of the tribal cultures there. As Crown fields and mines sprang up on the eastern coasts of North and South America and in the Caribbean, indigenous people were either massacred, enslaved, or pushed westward.

Meanwhile, in Mozambique and Madagascar the East India Company was busy rounding up tribal people into slavery and transporting them to work their newly-found India and Indonesia fiefdoms. But slaves weren't the only thing the East India Company shipped.

By the 19th century, the company was illegally selling opium in China to finance its Indian tea purchases. Lord Shelbourne launched the Chinese opium trade in 1783 with Scottish merchants from the East India Company and members of the Knights of St. John Jerusalem. By 1788, the Crown had established Freemason lodges in China. One, known as the Triad Society, would traffic their opium.

Opposition to this smuggling operation resulted in the First and Second Opium Wars in China between 1839 and 1860. British forces came to the rescue, winning both wars and ensuring that cheap Chinese tea would continue steaming into the markets of London and Antwerp. Both expeditions were led by Lord Palmerston, head of Scottish Rite Freemasonry in the UK.

Following defeat in the First Opium War, the Qing bloodline dynasty ceded yet another strategic island in the annals of history – Hong Kong – to the British in the 1842 Treaty of Nanjing. Following victory in the Second Opium War in 1860, the British got control over Kowloon. Later, they signed a 99-year lease on the New Territories, the third part of what we know as Hong Kong.

From this new Crown colony, the royals and their landed gentry would operate their Asian drug smuggling operation for the next 150 years. They would also come to base their shipping empire here with the formation of the Peninsular & Oriental Steam Navigation

Company (P&O) in 1837. By 1847, in the midst of the Opium Wars, the company was transporting Bengali opium into China.

Although headquartered in London, Hong Kong quickly became the global shipping hub for the P&O Group. Controlled by the Swire, Baring, and Inchcape families, it became the world's largest shipping company. The Swire's also control Hong Kong-based Cathay Pacific Airlines. P&O worked hand in glove with Hong Kong Shanghai Bank Corporation (HSBC) in facilitating the opium trade right up through the Vietnam War.

Much of the opium was shipped into Vancouver in Crown-controlled Canada where it was distributed through the P&O-controlled Hudson Bay Company and a string of new "China towns", which were popping up all along the west coast. Chinese coolie slaves were also shipped west to build JP Morgan's railroads into the US interior.

In 1997, P&O merged with the Dutch House of Orange-controlled Royal Nedlloyd to form P&O Nedlloyd Container Line Limited. In 2005, this company was absorbed by the Danish A.P. Moller-Maersk Group. Finally, in 2006 P&O's port or terminal business was sold to Dubai Ports, also known as DP World, which is controlled by the royal Al Maktoum family of Dubai.

HSBC was founded in Hong Kong in 1865 when Cantonese opium trafficker William Jardine combined forces with his fellow Anglo-Scot *hongs*, the Keswicks and William Sutherland Matheson, to form Jardine Matheson. The families then launched HSBC after the second Opium War as a repository for their opium proceeds. HSBC is now a subsidiary of the London-based HSBC Holdings, which today prints 75% of Hong Kong's currency, while the Cecil Rhodes-founded Standard Chartered Bank prints the rest. HSBC's Hong Kong headquarters sits next to a massive Masonic Temple.

Slavery was winding down and being replaced by slightly more subtle techniques that the royal bloodline would employ to run their global plantations – colonialism and capitalism. The latter included smuggling.

In 1991, HSBC moved its global headquarters to the City of London and by 2021, it had over $11 trillion in assets. It is Europe's largest bank and the eighth-largest bank in the world. Recently, HSBC was fined for laundering money for the Mexican drug cartels.

Interestingly, HSBC and Standard Chartered rule the financial roost today in Dubai, which has taken the place of Hong Kong as the Crown's global smuggling headquarters. Yesterday's Golden Triangle is today's Golden Crescent (Afghanistan & Pakistan) in terms of opium production. Dubai is much closer in proximity to this region.

It doesn't hurt that their monarchy-owned DP World handles 10% of all global container traffic in more than 40 countries. These world ports remain the hub through which the vast majority of the world's drugs, arms, gold, diamonds, oil, and humans are smuggled.

Colonialism had paralleled slavery for centuries. Led by the East India Company, the 19th century saw the apex of British mercantilism. But following the old Crown tradition of issuing papal bulls, colonization, and mercantilism, though not quite plumbing the depths like slavery, needed moral justification.

With their Enlightenment fraud gathering steam, the bloodline would now turn to the scientists rather than the church for rationalization of its heavy-handed economic models. Hoping to comfort and to trick guilt-ridden slave drivers and disgruntled serfs alike, they marched out a Scottish economist named Adam Smith to refine the notion and proclaim capitalism to be the world's superior economic system.

Smith worked for the East India Company. His 1776 book, *Wealth of Nations,* became Lord Shelbourne's bible as he prosecuted his Chinese opium wars. The East India Company spearhead would morph into Chatham House, which houses the Royal Institute for International Affairs – a parent company of the US Council on Foreign Relations. The names had changed, but the bloodline stayed the same.

From their City of London headquarters, the royals would concentrate their efforts going forward on concealing their power, launching a series of "scientific" institutions, funding certain pro-capitalist philosophers, and transforming the brutish East India Company into the more gentile and refined Chatham House.

In the mid-1800s, British East India Company General, Henry Rawlinson, a close associate of Lionel Rothschild, Cecil Rhodes, and Alfred Milner, unearthed more than thirty tons of documents from the Sumerian region near what is now Mosul, Iraq. Many of these were cuneiform contracts from the Babylonian era. They transported the documents to Basra, where the Tigris and Euphrates Rivers empty into the Persian Gulf, then built ships to transport the mother lode back to London, Paris, and Berlin.

Historians tell us that these ships were sunk as they set sail. By who, they do not say. Interestingly, following the late 20th century Gulf War, the British and the Crown's BP came to control Basra once again.

Chapter 9

Hobbes, Malthus, and Locke

While P&O was laundering Vancouver opium proceeds through HSBC, State Street First Boston was making a fortune on the transatlantic slave trade and the cotton and tobacco windfall it produced. The stockholder families became known collectively as the Boston Brahmin. These included the Lehman, Sutherland, Perkins, and Forbes families.

The genocide of Native Americans continued apace, as Crown mercenaries like Daniel Boone, Davy Crockett, and Kit Carson pushed west, regularly delivering their scalps to the proper authorities for a head-count of their kill. But not everything was going the bloodline's way.

On May 10, 1773, the British passed the Tea Act, which allowed the British East India Company to sell cheap Chinese tea without paying import taxes to the US colony. On December 16, 1773, a group of Boston merchants calling themselves the Sons of Liberty boarded an East India ship and destroyed its entire cargo of tea, tossing much of it into Boston Harbor.

This event became known as the Boston Tea Party and would serve as a clarion call for the 1776 American Revolution. Ironically, the protesters were disguised as Indians. Their nemesis, King George III, who ruled the House of Hanover, came from the Saxe-Gotha bloodline. A decade later, the French would launch their own revolution, deposing and beheading King Louis XVI of the powerful Bourbon bloodline.

The Crown had, through slavery, genocide and drug smuggling, accumulated massive amounts of wealth. But these revolutions made them nervous. They knew they needed to spruce up their image.

By the 16th century, Sir Francis Bacon and Thomas Hobbes had been the first in a steady stream of pro-monarchist British philosophers whose dark views were popularized by the bloodline to justify its ongoing global pillage.

They were followed by empiricists John Locke, David Hume, and Adam Smith, whose Wealth of Nations aggrandizement of capitalism was published the same year the American Revolution began. Next came 19th century utilitarians such as Jeremy Bentham, John Stuart Mill, and Thomas Malthus.

While there were slight differences in their philosophies, they all projected a dark wetiko view of human nature and of nature itself. All deemed free trade, mercantilism, and capitalism to be just the tonic for a brutish world that needed to be brought to heel. And all were pro-monarchy.

Best known for his 1581 book, *Leviathan,* Thomas Hobbes graduated from the usual bloodline UK universities of Oxford and Cambridge. He then became a tutor to William Cavendish, the son of William Cavendish, Baron of Hardwick, and later, the Earl of Devonshire. He later tutored William's son, also named William.

The Cavendish family became patrons of Hobbes, especially William III, who became 1st Duke of Newcastle who once organized an army for King Charles I during the English Civil War. Later, Hobbes would serve as math instructor to Charles, Prince of Wales.

Hobnobbing with royalty clearly influenced Thomas Hobbes' worldview. He once wrote, "The condition of man...is a condition of war of everyone against everyone." But was this a condition of man or of the Anunnaki hybrids he hung out with?

To Hobbes, life was "nasty, brutish and short." So at least for the subjects and slaves that his Cavendish family friends profited from.

"Force and fraud are in war the two cardinal virtues," Hobbes wrote. "Covenants without the sword are but words and of no strength to secure a man at all. When all the world is overcharged with inhabitants, then the last remedy of all is war, which provideth for every man, by victory or death".

This last sentence must have been music to the ears of the bloodlines, who would soon become obsessed with population control. On this front they found their chief mouthpiece in the form of Thomas Malthus.

In his 1798 book, *An Essay on the Principle of Population*, Malthus argued that improved standards of living, such as an increase in food production, would only lead to overpopulation. This view became popularized as the Malthusian trap.

Malthus criticized Britain's late 16th century Poor Laws on these grounds. These were the beginnings of the modern welfare state. Malthus failed to predict the efficiencies developed during the Industrial Revolution. But he had many proponents of his obsession with overpopulation, most notably Charles Darwin, whose expeditions were also patronized and influenced by the Crown.

Malthus' grandfather was Daniel Graham, apothecary to Kings George II and George III. Thomas graduated from Cambridge in 1791 and later took orders in the Church of England. In 1805, he became Professor of History and Political Economy at East India Company College in Hertfordshire. And in 1818, he became a fellow with the Royal Society.

Malthus' worldview was even darker than that of Hobbes. He particularly despised the poor. He once declared, "Instead of recommending cleanliness to the poor, we should encourage contrary habits. In our towns we should make the streets narrower, crowd more people into the houses, and court the return of the plague."

He added, "The redundant population, necessarily occasioned by the prevalence of early marriages, must be repressed by occasional famines, and by the custom of exposing children, which, in times of distress, is probably more frequent than ever acknowledged by Europeans."

Malthus is seen as the father of the eugenics movement, his diatribes often aimed at the poor and dark-skinned races. "It may at first appear strange", wrote Malthus, "but I believe it is true, that I cannot by means of money raise a poor man and enable him to live much better that he did before, without proportionably depressing others in the same class."

Malthus' views can be summed up with his statement, "Evil exists in the world not to create despair but activity." Malthus, like Hobbes and Locke and the others before him, was an apologist for the evil that their Royal Society pals were spreading around the world – an evil that had not existed on this planet prior to the Sumerian intervention.

It an amazing reflection of the power of the royal bloodline that the dark philosophies of their proteges are still being taught with any seriousness at major universities in this country and around the Western world. Their demonic views of nature and humanity have been thoroughly discredited by new scientists in a variety of fields, not least of which is the study of cultural anthropology.

The evil for which Hobbes, Locke, Smith, and Malthus served as apologists had by 1660 come to the "scientific" forefront with the formation of the Royal Society, also known as the Royal Society of London for Improving Natural Knowledge. One can immediately observe the oxymoron within the name of these urbanized, parochial, and extremely well-funded isolates from nature.

It has indeed proven very difficult for these chaps to understand the nature of reality from their City of London backbenches. Nevertheless, the foundation of the Royal Society began a period of what mainstream Crown-funded "science" terms the Enlightenment, which featured royal shills such as Cambridge graduate and Royal Society President, Sir Isaac Newton, along with Voltaire, and Oxford graduate and Royal Society member, John Locke.

Locke served as Secretary of the Board of Trade & Plantations, then as Secretary to the Lord's Proprietors of Carolina. A Lord's Proprietor was a person who was granted a royal charter to establish and govern an English colony. After a stint in the Netherlands, Locke accompanied Queen Mary II back to England.

Locke was an investor and a beneficiary of the Royal Africa Company, which was founded the same year as the Royal Society in 1660 by the House of Stuart monarchy and City of London merchants to ship slaves from West Africa to the Americas. This evil enterprise was led by the Duke of York, who would eventually become King James II.

The Royal Africa Company shipped more transatlantic slaves than any other company in history and was owned entirely by the British Crown, with King James II owning the majority. The establishment of the Royal Society that same year can be seen as scientific cover for a historic genocide undertaken by the Crown. Yet, it rationalizes their bad behavior to this day.

While the Enlightenment is portrayed as some sort of revolt against religion, it was simply another strategy of a bloodline that had converted to and promoted Protestantism since the Knights Templar falling out with the Catholic Church.

Now, scrapping all pretense of piety, they would claim open allegiance instead to science, which they found could be used to rationalize their actions even better than religion. It was the beginning of their Luciferian coming-out party and it is no coincidence that it paralleled the rapid spread of Freemasonry.

The Royal Society's ideas were now to be held superior to any silly notions of a Creator or God. The Nephilim fallen angels' ancient worship of their own intellect and disregard for the natural laws that God laid down, was now out in the open. But it was the Royal Society's job to make sure it would now slowly become a global religion open to all initiates.

Chapter 10

The Royal Society

Founded by royal charter in 1660, the Royal Society is the world's oldest continuous scientific academy. It was preceded by what was known as The Invisible College, which is mentioned in German Rosicrucian papers from the 17th century. A blueprint for the Royal Society was laid out in Sir Francis Bacon's fictional House of Solomon. In 1710, it set up shop at Crane Court on Fleet Street in the City of London. It has since relocated to Carlton House Terrace in Westminster.

Its branches include the Royal Society of Chemistry, Royal Society of Medicine, Royal Society of Arts, Royal Society of Biology, Royal Academy, Royal Institution of Chartered Surveyors, Royal Aeronautical Society, Royal Anthropological Institute, Royal Astronomical Society, Royal Economic Society, Royal Historical Society, Royal Pharmaceutical Society, Royal Entomological Society, Royal Geographical Society, Royal Society of Literature, Royal Horticultural Society, Royal Meteorological Society, Royal Statistical Society, Royal African Society, and Royal Asiatic Society.

This is only a partial list and there are many others spread throughout the Commonwealth. As you can see, the seven sacred sciences are all covered here. Probably the most powerful of these is the Royal Institute of International Affairs (RIIA), also known as Chatham House. Founded in 1920, its stated mission is to provide commentary on world events and offer solutions to global challenges.

In fact, it is the driving force when it comes to the foreign policy of the UK and its Commonwealth underlings. Its US affiliate is the Council on Foreign Relations, which serves the same role in shaping US foreign policy. Other national affiliates do the same – including the Australian Institute of International Affairs, Canadian International Council, German Council on Foreign Relations, Netherlands Institute of International Relations, Pakistan Institute of International Affairs, and the Singapore Institute of International Affairs.

The current obsession at Chatham House is support for arming Ukraine in the war against Russia. Prior to that, it was instrumental in shaping Covid-19 lockdown policies and vaccination mandates around the world. It works closely with the Royal United Services Institute (RUSI), the world's oldest defense and security think tank, founded in 1831 by Duke of Wellington Sir Arthur Wellesley, who descended from the old Venetian banker Welser clan. The current president of RUSI is Prince Edward, Duke of Kent, who openly backed Adolf Hitler.

While RIIA and RUSI shape and defend the imperialist policies of Britain and its allies, the Royal Geographic Society (RGS) is there to bolster those policies through its Malthusian views on human nature. Founded just one year before RUSI in 1830, RGSs mission was to keep tabs on the colonies and to absorb the Palestine Association, African Association, and Raleigh Club into its ranks. King William IV was the original patron, while the current royal patron is Princess Anne. In 1859, Queen Victoria granted it a royal charter.

RGS funded the expeditions of Charles Darwin, David Livingstone, Sir Edmund Hillary, and many other colonial explorers. Its mouthpiece magazines include *Geographical* and *National Geographic*. Within these pages, the reader often finds nature portrayed as a brutish place where competition and fighting are a constant theme.

RSG popularized the notion of survival of the fittest, skewing the central findings of Darwin's travels, which were – if a species was to survive, there must be extensive cooperation within that species, rather than competition. This junk science is often employed to defend Crown capitalism, which is ostensibly more "fit" than the countries they pilfer cheap labor and resources from.

I grew up on a farm. I hunted, fished, and trapped. Later, I did extensive back-country hiking in grizzly bear habitat in Montana, Idaho, and Wyoming. I've traveled to fifty countries and encountered wild animals in many of them, including a self-guided safari in South Africa's Kruger National Park. For most of my life I have lived in remote areas teeming with wildlife.

My scientific observation through it all is how little competition and fighting there is in both wild and domesticated animals. What I have seen is extensive cooperation, within species as well as across species. But this truism does nothing to defend the Crown's bad behavior, so the many scientists who have come to the same conclusion will receive no funding from the Royal Geographic Society.

It would have been easy in 18th-century London, having come through the Black Death and now in the middle of the Industrial Revolution, to view life as difficult and "brutish". Persians and Arabs traveling to the UK were appalled at the squalor they found. But this was not the original human condition, rather a result of living under a greedy and acquisitive monarchy, which always required an underclass to maintain its lavish lifestyle.

Agriculture had disrupted the natural relationships that mankind held dear for hundreds of thousands of years. Now the Industrial Revolution in Britain would take humans even further from these bonds, as farmers were lured into the cities with the promise of better paying factory jobs.

From 1760 to 1840, using raw materials pilfered by the East India Company from Asia, the Industrial Revolution gathered pace in the UK. Steam and water power were used to produce iron and manufacture chemicals. The textile industry led the way as Crown factories hired desperate serfs to work their new machines. Much of the cotton and dyes came from Bengal.

From 1870 to 1915, the Second Industrial Revolution occurred. Machine tools were developed, standardization became entrenched, interchangeable parts were common, and mass production became possible. Railroads and telegraph lines swept across Europe, water and sewer systems were modernized, and oil was discovered and utilized as a new power source.

A Third Industrial Revolution occurred in the mid-20th century, featuring the replacement of analog and mechanical systems with electronic, digital, and eventually computerized ones. This marked the beginning of the Information Age.

The second focus of the Royal Geographic Society is to tell us how we evolved from the Great Apes. Though it is certainly a possibility, their evolutionary theory has yet to be proven in this regard. The fossil record is incomplete, the effectiveness of carbon dating has come under increased scrutiny, and the "missing link" between Great Apes and humans has yet to be established.

For decades, *Ramapithecus* was paraded around by Crown-funded anthropologists at Yale led by Elwyn Simons as the missing link. But research by biochemist Allan Wilson and Berkeley anthropologist, Vincent Sarich, led a group of scientists in challenging this belief. Though initially dismissed by the mainstream scientific community, the mounting evidence that *Ramapithecus* was, in fact, *Sivapithecus* (the ancestor to orangutans), became overwhelming and even Simons was forced to admit his error.

Despite this new scientific discovery, many otherwise highly-educated people in the world still believe in evolutionary theory as gospel. This Crown-driven junk science has indeed become their new religion.

Similarly, the Royal Society of Physics had driven the particle physics train for centuries, informing us that all matter was made up of highly predictable elementary particles called atoms. This belief had existed since the 6th century. But starting in the 19th century many began to question this orthodoxy, giving rise to subatomic physics.

It began with scientists identifying positively-charged protons and neutral neutrons. Smaller and smaller particles were identified, but their actions were not at all predictable. This understanding developed into quantum field theory, which maintained that particles and their interactions were the same since their movements could even be affected by the mood of the experimenter. Sir Isaac Newton's Crown-funded laws were quickly unraveling.

In the 1950s, particle accelerators like CERN were developed to try to smash the smaller and smaller particles like quarks and leptons into one another to find even smaller ones. This very expensive madness has resulted in new theories like the unified field theory and string theory, which revolve around Higgs boson, popularized as the God particle, after a book of the same name by Nobel Laureate Leon Lederman of Crown-controlled Columbia University.

But a new science alternative to particle physics has emerged which focuses on matter that consists of electricity rather than particles. This new plasma physics has made serious inroads at major universities, where it is now taught that there are four states of matter: solid, liquid, gas, and plasma. David Talbot and his Thunderbolt Project are pioneers in this field.

Talbot's discoveries also carry over into astronomy, another of the Nephilim's always-inverted seven sacred sciences. The Royal Astronomical Society has espoused the Big Bang Theory, which uses particle physics theories and Einstein's theory of relativity to posit that the universe was created in one massive explosion.

Talbot and his plasma physics ilk have challenged this theory, finding that the universe is electric, plasma-based, and ever-changing. They argue that most of what has transpired in the creation of the universe is not based on collisions or explosions, but on electrical charges caused by cosmic lightning storms.

One cannot escape the pattern that emerges from the Crown's "science" in trying to explain things like the origin of man, what constitutes matter, and how the universe was created. Their conclusions in these areas involve explanations that tend to diminish mankind, to atomize and dissect reality, and to explain away Wakan

Tanka's mysterious creation as resulting from random, chaotic, and violent events in the universe.

Again, they are projecting their dark worldview into their new scientific Trojan Horse as a means to discourage humanity from the possibility of real progress. Rather than seeing what is actually in front of them, they instead reflect in their findings a colonizer mindset, bent on proving the superiority of the bloodline at the expense of nature, humans, and even God.

Hatched in Babylon as an Anunnaki means to control humans, religion and spirituality had been well-utilized by the Crown to maintain control of their Holy Roman Empire. But the Catholic Church had renounced the Templar knights of the Crown as heretics, and Protestantism wasn't injected with enough guilt and shame to keep the peasants in line. Judaism could and would still be mobilized occasionally, but only to garner sympathy from the public when required.

The answer to maintaining control over the growing global population lie in the Royal Societies and their Malthusian, bloodline supremacist, dark view of the world. They had already destroyed human relationships with nature in their push to enslave humans into agriculture. Now they would push them into cities to work at Crown corporations. An urbanized population is a scared population, and one more likely to adopt such dark views as to the nature of reality.

Better to rid the world of any notion of a supreme and benevolent Creator, though they had done their best to portray God as angry and quick to condemn. Now they would go back to their Sumerian and Egyptian pagan roots and coerce populations by the sword and by science, inverting the Nephilim fallen angel's seven sacred sciences to assuage humanity to acquiesce to their continued tyranny.

Chapter 11

First-Strike Wetiko

Religion and science simply serve as propaganda mechanisms through which the royal Anunnaki bloodline can usurp moral authority and control humanity. Laws and governments can then carry out their mandates without much outcry. But in the end, it is through brute force that the Crown has always maintained and expanded its geopolitical power.

Around 1650, the East India Company began to ship saltpeter from Bengal into England. An essential ingredient in gunpowder, the saltpeter trade grew steadily, experiencing a huge spike during the Crown-sponsored US Civil War.

Gunpowder can be seen as possibly the most important discovery in history for the Crown. It gave a whole new meaning to their neo-Darwinian "survival of the fittest" credo since now strength, speed, and agility had little to do with winning a battle. It was all about who had the most guns and ammunition. And it was no coincidence that the British Empire took off with the discovery of saltpeter.

The new credo for Pax Britannica was "might is right". And in the hands of these wetiko psychopaths it was shoot first, ask questions later. During the nuclear era, this doctrine would become known as a "first-strike option". That first-strike mentality was one of the many destructive "gifts" that the Anunnaki "gods" bestowed upon the human race.

Humans devolved from hunter-gatherers, to agriculturalists, to downright paranoid city-dwellers. Many adopted this first-strike mindset, which not by coincidence, meshed perfectly with the Crown's capitalist and colonialist ways. It was also good for gun sales.

This first-strike wetiko is rooted in a fear of nature and a doubt as to the goodness of human nature. It is, at its core, a misunderstanding as to the nature of reality, where reciprocity and relationships matter more than competition and conquest. You could also call it Satanism.

In his book, *The Way of the Human Being*, former Rutgers history professor, Calvin Luther Martin gets to the core of this first-strike insanity. Martin spent time with both the Navajo and the Yupik people, learning far more than he ever learned at any Crown-funded university.

He uses the example of a European explorer, most likely funded by one of the monarchs of Europe. The man was hunting in Alaska when he came upon a brown bear. The bear was still quite a distance away and showed no aggression toward the hunter. But instead of talking to the bear and asking permission to pass its way without conflict, which any Yupik hunter/scientist would have done, the man simply raises his rifle in fear and shoots the bear dead, later bragging about his "bravery" and mounting the stuffed corpse as a trophy to his fear upon a palace wall in Europe.

He wasn't educated enough to know that he had just fractured the entire relationship between bears and humans. He wasn't brave enough to stand his ground while talking the bear away. He wasn't man enough to let the bear live and go back to its family. Instead, he was a wetiko coward, well-trained by the Crown colonizers that had displayed these same traits over and over as they ransacked the planet for centuries.

All because they didn't understand the nature of reality.

Humans did not act this way for hundreds of thousands of years. They only began acting this way after the Anunnaki intervention in Sumeria, which forced them into agriculture and away from any relationships they had with the natural world. The bloodline's first-strike mentality has been on display ever since they landed here and it is the biggest clue that they are indeed not human. They came from a place of conflict in the universe and they brought with them the fear and mistrust which that conflict instilled in them.

Fast forward to today and you can see the carnage and misery that this dark Satanic mentality has wrought upon the human race. Divorce is rampant because many couples enter relationships with this mentality. The minute something goes wrong they get scared and defensive, blaming the other, while taking no responsibility for their role in the problem.

Paranoid Western governments sanction other governments whose policies aren't in line with global Crown hegemony, often funding violent mercenaries to destabilize or even topple these independent states. Negotiation only occurs after the mercenaries have created enough carnage to gain an upper hand. Everything is calculated, not for peace and harmony, but for "victory". But these are short-lived. Inevitably, the people remember what happened to them and rise up once again against neocolonialism and tyranny.

Conquest over nature is also short-lived. This is witnessed in our modern day by mass animal extinctions, the Mississippi River drying up, famines around the world, out-of-control geoengineered weather, and the like.

Martin tells another story in his book about a Yupik Eskimo hunter who got lost while hunting caribou. He eventually collapsed in the snow from exhaustion. A pack of arctic foxes came by and laid down beside him, surrounding him with warmth and keeping him alive until the weather had cleared and he regained his strength. The hunter told Martin that after this incident he was able to trap arctic foxes whenever he needed to. By understanding the reciprocal and relational nature of reality, this Yupik hunter thrived and had a rich life.

We are told by Crown media shills that their confrontational delusions are necessary in such an unpredictable and dangerous world because, after all, we are dealing with "human nature". How many times have you heard a person in the past week repeat this

Malthusian lie in saying, "Well, we're only human", or "It's just human nature".

In truth, people who do bad things are not human enough. Jesus said we are all divine sons and daughters of God. Native people have no concept of original sin. It was the Crown-controlled Council of Nicaea that literally changed Jesus' words and deemed him the sole unattainable messiah, lowering the bar for the rest of us to stay human.

We come out of our mother's womb perfect. But almost immediately, the socialization into Crown-thought begins. Parents, teachers, friends, and acquaintances have all been initiated into the Royal Society perception-control grid. So they all unwittingly further the bloodline mind control by repeating misconceptions as to the nature of reality. They are Satanists, but sadly they do not know this.

This results in a deep-seated fear and mistrust of both the natural world and other humans. It also results in latent self-hatred, which the Crown loves to have humans carry around all through their lives. A human who hates themselves is rendered impotent as a force of change in the world. Their ability to see and then challenge bloodline control over their lives is stifled. And they tend to shop more at the Crown's malls and big box stores, forever trying to fill the void of a narcissistic, isolated, and self-loathing existence.

Isolation is the key to maintaining the Crown control grid. We went from hunter-gatherers to agriculturalists to city dwellers, with an increase in social isolation every step of the way. Tribes became extended families became nuclear families became broken single-parent families in a matter of just a few thousand years. And now we are being further isolated and targeted by their internet and "social media", which was designed by Crown intelligence assets to create division, hatred, and chaos, ensuring further social isolation.

The Anunnaki royals have always utilized the lizard brain portion of their cerebral cortex. Everything to them is reductionist. Everything must be broken apart, atomized, put under a microscope, categorized, classified, defined, and named. Their version of objectivity makes their science a fraud from the outset. No two creatures will act alike in any given situation. Nature versus nurture is just another of their dualistic fallacies. Dualism itself simply sets up an unnecessary conflict. Like Harvey Wall Banger, Silent Bob, and Slow Loris, we are all unique individual souls. Therefore, our behavior is extremely subjective and unpredictable.

In the same way, the CERN mad scientists are painfully and expensively finding out that matter and tiny particles are also very unpredictable. You cannot gain a better understanding of the nature of reality by isolating things and breaking them down to their smallest component. It is just the opposite. You begin to understand the nature of reality when you zoom out and see the world as a living breathing organism that in the end, minus stupid human intervention, acts unpredictably and yet paradoxically in circular unison.

Much of the joy of life comes not in the knowing of things, but in the humility that there is far more about the universe that we don't know. This is why the best things in life often happen unexpectedly and without planning. Synchronicity and serendipity occur in an intellectual vacuum where calculation and cunning are absent. This is the story of the Tree of Life in the Garden of Eden tale, where intellectual self-deception trumped gratitude and acceptance.

Those who claim expertise are often the most scarred by the fear and mistrust pushed like heroin by the bloodline wetiko. They cling to their titles and the power it gives them, but most are useful idiots to the Crown agenda. They live miserable lives of bondage to a warped value system and subject the rest of us to their wetiko neurosis since these types become leaders in all areas of society. The Babylon system ensures this.

Those who refuse to comply with this inverted Luciferian reality are deemed revolutionaries or, more recently, "conspiracy theorists". They are the people who have, at some level, seen through the wetiko veil. Often cast as paranoid, they are, ironically, the least paranoid among us as they attempt to remain true to their human roots. While most of society remains reactionary and fearful, willing to go along with this radical departure from reality that the Crown hides behind, the revolutionary trusts humanity while loathing the Crown system.

Paradoxically, the more you love humanity, the more you must hate the system. Most people buy into the Satanism. They hate humanity and love the unjust system. We are taught that there is no difference between the nature of humanity and the nature of the system. This is why your local nightly news reports on all manner of crimes committed by average citizens while never covering crimes committed by the elite who control the system.

The first-strike mentality is portrayed in nearly every single movie, documentary, newscast, and television drama we are shown. This is no accident. The screen has replaced the radio and newspaper as the Crown's main propaganda delivery device. Edward Bernays' work and the whole cybernetic movement have refined bloodline messaging down to a science. Their CIA MK-Ultra experiments are now being carried out on a mass scale and the whole of humanity is their subject.

They have to keep people in a reactive state of fear because this produces isolation and division. Divide and conquer has been the primary royal bloodline strategy for controlling humanity ever since they arrived in this Garden of Eden. Usury has been a close second.

Chapter 12

The Bloodline Take Down of America: Part I

During the American Revolution, many Crown agents were trying to steer the outcome in favor of the hated Crown. The Crown's Freemason "knights" had already established lodges in the colonies to this end. Many scholars believe that the American Revolution was allowed to happen since the British Parliament would no longer control the US, but through various mechanisms, the Crown could still exert control. The most important of these mechanisms was usury, which they controlled through their cartel banks. Indeed, the US national debt now stands at $31.5 trillion.

When the US was founded, there was a big debate over whether or not we should have a public or a private central bank. Arguing on the side of a public bank were people like Thomas Jefferson, John Adams, John Quincy Adams, and James Monroe. None were Freemasons. On the other side, arguing for a privately-owned bank were George Washington, John Jay, Benjamin Franklin, and Alexander Hamilton. All were high-level Freemasons.

Hamilton was also acting as a Crown agent on behalf of the Rothschild family, bankers to the British Crown. The Freemasons won out and in 1789, Alexander Hamilton became the first US Treasury Secretary. But the real power would be wielded by the new Rothschild-controlled private central bank – the Bank of the United States – which was founded in 1791.

Hamilton, who also went on to found the powerful Bank of New York (now Bank of New York Mellon), exemplified the contempt that his long-indoctrinated Freemason faction held for humanity, once stating, "All communities divide themselves into the few and the many. The first are the rich and the well-born, the others the mass of the people...The people are turbulent and changing; they seldom judge and determine right. Give therefore to the first class a distinct, permanent share of government. They will check the unsteadiness of the second."

Thomas Jefferson replied to this nonsense, "A country which expects to remain ignorant and free...expects that which has never been and that which will never be. There is scarcely a King in a hundred who would not, if he could, follow the example of Pharaoh – get first all the people's money, then all their lands, and then make them and their children servants forever...banking establishments are more dangerous than standing armies. Already they have raised up a money aristocracy."

Nevertheless, the Bank of the United States held its 20-year charter until 1811. Public opposition to the bank was strong, but the Crown plunged the country into the War of 1812, through which the US accrued debt to the Bank of the United States (BUS). With the country facing economic ruin, the Bank's charter was renewed in 1816.

In 1828, Andrew Jackson ran for President on an anti-BUS platform railing, "You are a den of vipers. I intend to expose you and by Eternal God I will rout you out. If the people understood the rank injustices of our money and banking system there would be a revolution before morning."

Jackson won the election and immediately revoked the BUS charter saying, "The Act seems to be predicated on an erroneous idea that the present shareholders have a prescriptive right to not only the favor, but the bounty of the government...for their benefit does this Act exclude the whole American people from competition in the purchase of this monopoly. Present stockholders and those inheriting their rights as successors be established a privileged order, clothed both with great political power and enjoying immense pecuniary advantages from their connection with government. Should its influence be concentrated under the operation of such an Act as this, in the hands of a self-elected directory whose interests are identified with those of the foreign stockholders, will there not be cause to tremble for the independence of our country in war...controlling our currency, receiving our public monies and holding thousands of our citizens' independence, it would be more formidable and dangerous than the naval and military power of the enemy. It is to be regretted that the rich and powerful too often bend the acts of government for selfish purposes...to make the rich richer and more powerful. Many of our rich men have not been content with equal protection and equal benefits, but have besought us to make them richer by acts of Congress. I have done my duty to this country."

In 1835, Jackson was the target of the first assassination attempt on a US President. The gunman was Richard Lawrence, who confessed that he was "in touch with the powers in Europe". But under Jackson's leadership, the US national debt went to zero for the first and last time in our history.

Enraged by Jackson's opposition to Crown usury, BUS President Nicholas Biddle cut off funding to the US government in 1842, plunging America into a depression. Biddle's boss was the Paris-based Jacob Rothschild. Eager to expand their Southern slave trade into Mexico and Central America, the Crown also sprang the Mexican-American War on Jackson.

The Civil War began a short time later, with the Crown funding both sides in an attempt to destroy their unruly colony. They were also funding Emperor Maximilian I of Mexico to harass the US from the southern border. The Austrian was the Emperor of the Second Mexican Empire from 1864 to 1867. The archduke was also a member of the powerful House of Hapsburg-Lorraine. He was installed after the Crowns of Spain, France, and the UK invaded Mexico in 1861 over unpaid debt. By 1861, the US was $100 million in debt to the Crown.

But newly-elected President Abraham Lincoln showed a similar attitude towards Crown usury, issuing Lincoln Greenbacks to pay

Union Army bills. The Crown mouthpiece, the *Times of London*, now called for the "destruction of the US government".

The Euro-banker-written *Hazard Circular* was exposed and distributed throughout the country by angry populists. It said, "The European Bankers favor the end of slavery...the European plan is that capital money lenders shall control labor by controlling wages. The great debt that capitalists will see is made out of the war and must be used to control the valve of money. To accomplish this government bonds must be used as a banking basis. We are now awaiting the Secretary of Treasury Salmon Chase to make that recommendation. It will not allow Greenbacks to circulate as money as we cannot control that. We control bonds and through them banking issues".

The 1863 National Banking Act reinstated a private US central bank and Chase's war bonds were issued. Lincoln was re-elected the next year, vowing to repeal the act after he took his January 1865 oath of office. But before he could act, he was assassinated at the Ford Theater by John Wilkes Booth. Booth had major connections to the international bankers. His granddaughter wrote, *This One Mad Act*, which details Booth's contact with "mysterious Europeans" just before the Lincoln assassination.

Following the Lincoln hit, Booth was whisked away by members of a secret society known as the Knights of the Golden Circle (KGC). KGC had close ties to the French Society of Seasons, which produced Karl Marx. KGC had fomented much of the tension that caused the Civil War and President Lincoln had specifically targeted the group. Booth was a KGC member and was connected through the Confederate Secretary of State, Judah Benjamin, to the House of Rothschild. Benjamin fled to England after the war.

With the Second Bank of the United States in place and the global slave trade winding down, the Crown's global hegemony project entered a new phase. The colonial adventurers at the East India Company, the Royal Africa Company, and the P&O would be replaced by a team of Oxford and Cambridge-educated economists who would be put to work taking over and running central banks in every corner of the planet. The old colonialism of whips and chains would be replaced by a new more gentile variety involving bankers in suits. And usury would be central to the plan.

In 1871, President Ulysses S. Grant signed the Global Estate Trust Agreement with the international bankers. This made the United States a subsidiary corporation of the City of London Corporation. It also made each state a subsidiary of the United States Corporation, which under British Maritime Law, would be listed as a foreign entity based in the new jurisdiction called the District of Columbia.

The DC entity had been laid out using Freemason symbology and its separate legal offshore status was modeled after that of the City of London. Under the Global Estate Trust the City of London would remain the Crown's global financial center but the District of Columbia would become its global military power base, transforming the United States into a Hessianized mercenary force for global Crown interests.

During the Great Depression, the United States Corporation went bankrupt. And in 1933, the 33rd Degree Mason, President Franklin Delano Roosevelt, was forced to call in the entire gold holdings of the citizens of the United States as collateral on a new Crown loan. A Social Security system was established as part of Roosevelt's New Deal.

While the system was touted as a liberal advance in protecting the elderly, what it actually did was make every US citizen's birth certificate a tradable commodity on Wall Street and in the City, using their social security number as a way to track their productiveness or lack thereof. The industriousness of US citizens was now being used as additional collateral on all future Crown lending.

The groundwork for this was laid in 1913 as the Crown-controlled US Federal Reserve Bank replaced the Second Bank of the United States. This came just four years after the founding of the Business Roundtable in London in 1909 by Lord Nathan Rothschild, Lord Alfred Milner, and South African colonizer-extraordinaire, Cecil Rhodes. Rhodes founded DeBeers, that to this day remains a global diamond monopoly, as well as the old HongKong-turned-Dubai money laundry known as Standard Chartered Bank

The Business Roundtable hatched a plan to secretly extend Pax Britannica by allowing local elections, but continuing Crown control of nations through ownership of their respective central banks. The Business Roundtable essentially merged with remnants of the old East India Company to become Chatham House or the Royal Institute of International Affairs (RIIA), which was officially founded in 1920. The RIIA is a registered charity of the Crown.

According to former British Intelligence officer, John Coleman, who wrote, *The Conspirators' Hierarchy: The Committee of 300*, "Round Tablers armed with immense wealth from gold, diamond and drug monopolies fanned out throughout the world to take control of fiscal and monetary policies and political leadership in all countries where they operated."

While Cecil Rhodes and the Oppenheimers went to South Africa, the Kuhn Loebs were off to re-colonize America. Rudyard Kipling was sent to India, the Schiffs and Warburgs manhandled Russia, while the Rothschilds, Lazards, and Israel Moses Seifs pushed into the Middle East. In Princeton, New Jersey, the Round Table founded the Institute for Advanced Study (IAS) as a partner to its All Souls College at Oxford. IAS was funded by the Rockefeller's General Education Board.

IAS members Robert Oppenheimer, Neils Bohr, and Albert Einstein created the atomic bomb. Their twisted worldview called for breaking things apart rather than unifying them together so they chose nuclear fission over nuclear fusion, which could be, according to recent breakthroughs by new scientists, the key to producing free energy.

Six years later, after the formation of Chatham House in 1926 as part of this fake decolonization effort, the British Commonwealth of Nations was formed. Today this includes 56 nations, most of which were officially part of the British Empire. While touting itself as a boon to member nations, it actually leaves them firmly under City of London control since their official head of state is King Charles III. Recently there has been an exodus from the

Commonwealth by countries including Gambia, Guadeloupe, and Barbados.

It was President Woodrow Wilson who signed the 1913 Federal Reserve Act into law. Wilson's close friend Colonel Ely Garrison would later write in his book, *Roosevelt, Wilson and the Federal Reserve*, "Paul Warburg was the man who got the Federal Reserve Act together after the Aldrich Plan aroused such nationwide resentment and opposition. The mastermind of both plans was Baron Alfred Rothschild of London."

The first Chairman of the new Federal Reserve bank was none other than Paul Warburg of the German banking dynasty. His is one of eight families who, to this day, control the Federal Reserve. The others are Rockefeller, Rothschild, Goldman Sachs, Lazard, Kuhn Loeb, Israel Moses Seif, and Lehman/Oppenheimer.

Four years later, with the United States Corporation military wing already established, the US was lured into entering World War I after a secret society known as the Black Hand assassinated Archduke Ferdinand and his Hapsburg wife. The Archduke's friend Count Czerin later said, "A year before the war he informed me that the Masons had resolved upon his death."

That same year, Bolsheviks overthrew the Hohenzollern monarchy in Russia with help from Max Warburg and Jacob Schiff, while the Balfour Declaration leading to the creation of Israel was penned to Zionist Second Lord Rothschild. This was closely followed by the 1927 Treaty of Jeddah, which guaranteed that Saudi Arabia would recognize Crown protectorates Qatar, Bahrain, Oman, United Arab Emirates, and Kuwait, which later joined with the Saudis to form the Gulf Cooperation Council.

The year 1917 also saw the 16th Amendment added to the US Constitution, levying a national income tax even though it was ratified by only two of the required 36 states. The revenue gained from the income tax was to replace the excise taxes charged to Crown corporations doing business in the US. It was no coincidence that the Rockefeller Foundation was launched four years earlier when the Fed was formed. Through foundations, the Crown can both shield its wealth from taxation and socially engineer the general public.

By the mid-1930's oil had been discovered by Rockefeller's Chevron in Saudi Arabia. Coupled with the oil found earlier by the House of Orange-Nassau's Royal Dutch Shell in Azerbaijan, this cheap new energy source would power the efforts of the Round Table to maximize profits in their new Commonwealth fiefdom, using the bankrupt United States Corporation as their military enforcer.

The opium proved lucrative for the Crown, but oil would surpass it as the world's most profitable commodity. But it was a third industry that would eventually surpass both drugs and oil as the Crown's most important money machine – manufacturing the weapons of war, euphemistically known as the "defense" industry.

In my book, *Big Oil & Their Bankers in the Persian Gulf: Four Horsemen, Eight Families and their Global Intelligence, Narcotics and Terror Network,* I discuss in detail the City of London's control of these three most valuable commodities in the world.

The Rothschilds had already funded both sides of numerous European conflicts, from the Crimean War to the Napoleonic Wars to World War I. Now, with oil to burn, Germany spiraled into hyperinflation. And with the US needing the new industry coming out of the Goldman Sachs-engineered Great Depression, the Crown would light the fuse for their most ambitious military conflict yet – World War II.

In Japan, the royal Yamato bloodline had been Emperors for centuries, much to the chagrin of the average Japanese citizen. The royal shoguns were becoming increasingly unpopular and Japan's Communist Party was burgeoning in membership. Something had to be done to stave off a revolution.

The Crown began to groom Isoroku Yamamoto. Born Isoroku Takano, his father was a samurai from the Nagaoka feudal domain, which was ruled by the Makino clan. Samurai were hereditary nobility who protected the *daimyo* fiefdoms of the royal Nephilim bloodlines in Japan. Takano was adopted by the Yamamoto family in 1916 and quickly rose through the ranks of the Japanese Naval establishment.

From 1919-1921 he attended Harvard University, which along with Yale, would now serve the same role as Oxford and Cambridge in manufacturing loyal Crown Agents to run the United States Corporation. In 1924, he visited the US Naval War College. In 1930, now a rear admiral, he attended the London Naval Conference. Five years later, he turned up at the Second London Naval Conference.

Though these conferences were touted as olive branches to disarmament, just the opposite was happening in both Japan and the US where the Crown was building up its armament industry. In 1940, Yamamoto became an Admiral. And one year later, as commander-in-chief of the Combined Fleet, he was planning the infamous December 7, 1941 attack on Pearl Harbor.

Before this false flag event, the US public was strongly against entering WWII to help the Crown. But US President and 33rd Degree Mason, Franklin Delano Roosevelt, eventually performed his Masonic duty to the Crown and acceded to British Prime Minister and 33rd Degree Mason Winston Churchill's calls for help. Roosevelt ignored warnings that the Japanese fleet was headed for Hawaii, while quietly moving the most expensive military equipment out of Pearl Harbor ahead of the strikes.

Yamamoto had served his royal bloodline benefactors well. The terms demanded by General Douglas MacArthur in the peace agreement following WWII included leaving the royal Yamato family in place as official heads of state in Japan and banning the Japanese Communist Party. The bloodline-controlled *daimyo* would be re-branded as *zaibatsu*, six giant interlocking corporations that would lead the world through the electronics and digital-driven Third and Fourth Industrial Revolutions. Mitsubishi was organized from the Dan family *daimyo*, while Mitsui came from its namesake Mitsui family. The other four are Sumitomo, Daichikangin, Yasuda, and Nomura. These six companies own nearly every Japanese multinational corporation to this day.

Meanwhile, in Europe, the Crown was grooming two other wetiko warriors in their quest for another world war. The House of

Savoy, a royal dynasty founded in 1003, had unified Italy and ruled as monarchs through a succession of kings until King Umberto II finally stepped down in 1946, ending Italy's "official" rule by monarchy.

In 1922, House of Savoy King Victor Emmanuel III appointed self-proclaimed fascist Benito Mussolini as Prime Minister of Italy. Victor was also the King of Ethiopia and Albania for a time and the Savoy bloodline had also ruled Spain. In Italy, the Savoys stood by as Mussolini's *squadristi*, or Black Shirts, brutally attacked domestic enemies and built their National Fascist Party. Remember, it was the old Venetian bloodline bankers who had come up with the concept of fascism.

A year earlier in 1921, the newly-founded Royal Institute of International Affairs hatched the Tavistock Institute of Human Relations. Initially headed by military intelligence officer Major John Rawlings, Tavistock would become a false flag and social engineering incubator creating pretexts worldwide that required United States Corporation military intervention on behalf of the City of London's financial interests.

Isoroku Yamamoto and Benito Mussolini were two such walking, breathing pretexts. But before Tavistock was even officially founded the Crown invited a third such person for a visit – Adolf Hitler.

From February until November of 1912, Hitler attended the British Military Psych-ops School in both Devon and Ireland. This later became the Tavistock Institute. It is the psychological warfare arm of the Crown and is involved in everything from Hollywood to gang stalking. Shortly after its inception, the Tavistock began promoting the neo-Malthusian philosophies of Carl Jung and Sigmund Freud of the Frankfurt School.

By 1922, Queen Victoria's son Prince Charles Edward had met Adolf Hitler. In 1933, the prince became a member of the Nazi Party. He would soon become its leader. Several other royal family members supported Hitler and his Nazi Party, including Royal Dutch Shell insider, Prince Bernhard of the Dutch House of Orange-Nassau.

That same year, Prince Charles Edward became President of the German Red Cross, another Crown tentacle that funds its global spy operations by stealing the blood of "donors" and selling it to hospitals for hundreds of dollars per pint. Red Cross is simply the English language version of *Rosicrucians*, whose main job it is to guard the secret that the royal bloodline is not human. Red Cross refers to the crossing of blood between the Anunnaki and humankind. The reason Jesus had to die on a bloody red cross is because they wanted this revolutionary to suffer a slow tortuous crucifixion to symbolize the grafting of bloodlines, also referred to by those in the know as Zionism.

Chapter 13

The Royal Bloodline Command Structure

The Rosicrucians have a very important role in the Crown's concealment of its Anunnaki origins. But they are not at the top of the hierarchical pyramid that is the Nephilim Crown.

As we have seen, the single corrupted bloodline that controls the banking, politics, sciences, media, militaries, and educational institutions on this planet goes back at least 8,500 years to ancient Sumeria and Babylon. Their "royal" blood is the *Sangreal,* or Holy Grail, and is indeed different from that of humans. They are hybrids of the Nephilim, or fallen angels, from the Book of Genesis. Others call them Anunnaki. There blood is Rh-Negative, which less than 15% of the people on the planet have.

The Sangreal is their biggest secret, guarded closely by their secret society minions. It explains their obsession with blood types, genealogy, genome sequencing, and DNA mapping. At the very highest levels of the cabal, a Privy Council serves every monarch in the world. The Privy Council is also nobility since the Latin word *nobilitatis* means "high-ranking". The Crown recruits its Privy Council from the various sectors of society that it controls.

Possibly the most powerful bloodline is that of the Merovingian family which claims to descend from Oannes, a Nephilim hybrid abomination mentioned in the Babylonian texts, who came from the sea and was half fish and half man. The Merovingians also claim to descend from the Tribe of Dan, which settled at the base of Mt. Zion; and to Jesus, who they say was taken off the cross before death, married Mary Magdalene and had three children. The latter claim is a tactical lie that has garnered them sympathy via Dan Brown's propaganda books and films and will be utilized to justify their coming fake Second Coming of Christ.

The Merovingians morphed into the French Frank and Bourbon kings. These have intermarried, as all these bloodlines do, with the House of Hapsburg or Habsburg, who proudly display the Spear of Destiny that was used to kill Jesus at one of their Austrian castles. They were prominent among the Holy Roman Emperors.

King Juan Carlos of Spain has the surname de Borbon y Borbon, which is indicative of this interbreeding. Many members of the Hapsburg bloodline suffer various physical disfigurations, especially of the jaw. This comes from their obsession with inbreeding and is commonly known as the "Hapsburg jaw".

The Merovingians also bred the Smith & Sinclair, or St. Clair lineages. The former is the most common surname in America. The latter is a powerful bloodline that intermarried with the powerful Bruce lineage, eased the Knights Templar loot into the City of London banking system, and elevated modern-day Freemasonry. They own the famous Rosslyn Chapel in Scotland, which was founded in 1446 by Sr. William St. Clair and is legendary for its Rosicrucian, Knights Templar, and Freemason connections.

The Plantagenets are another powerful bloodline that intermarried with the French Anjou and the Norse Viking Rollo bloodline when the Normandy interbreeding frenzy occurred in the 14th and 15th centuries. These Normans then invaded the British Isles via William the Conqueror. Nearly every US President descends from Plantagenet royals. This is also the Charlemagne bloodline.

Charles the Great was part of the Carolingian dynasty. He became King of the Franks in 768 and King of the Lombards – the old Venetian banking family – in 774. In 800, he became the first Roman Emperor, known as Emperor Charlemagne.

Another powerful Anunnaki bloodline is the Indian Khan family – founders of Sufism, racehorse owners, and financiers of Islamic terror worldwide via their Crown charity Aga Khan Foundation. They descend from Genghis Khan's Mongol marauders who were used as mercenaries by the Venetian bankers in their wars against Constantinople.

The Chinese Li family controls the Triad mafia, which was founded by Freemasons at the East India Company. They proudly claim to descend from dragons. During the Tang dynasty, there were seven noble families: the Li family of Zhaojun, the Li family of Longxi, the Lu family of Fanyang, The Cui family of Bolin, the Cui family of Qinghe, and the Wang family of Taiyuan. The Tang Dynasty was founded by the Li family, which enriched itself by doing Silk Road trade with the Khazarian Ashkenazis.

The Yamato family are Japan's emperors. The Imperial House of Japan dates back to 660 BC. When Emperor Hirohito sent young Japanese on kamikaze missions against the US in WWII, they were told that they were truly "wind from the Gods". The House of Yamato and many Japanese believe they descend from the wind goddess, Ameretsu. The Shinto religion that predominates in Japan perpetuates this nonsense.

The Rothschild family – formerly the Bauers and Baccarats – are Talmudic Babylonians turned Khazarian Ashkenazi "Jews" who spent time as accountants for the German House of Hesse and became bankers to many European monarchs before intermarrying into the bloodlines. They probably changed their name to Rothschild because it means "red shield". Just as the Rosicrucians protect the bloodline secret that the royals are not human, the Rothschilds serve as a shield for the bloodline when it comes to pesky researchers of the global elite.

Many researchers place the Rothschilds at the top of the global power pyramid. And while they are very powerful, they specialize in banking, which is but one component of the Crown's global control apparatus. More importantly, they shield the rest of the bloodline from public view and the resulting criticism. They are known as the red shield, or bloodline shield.

According to prominent researchers like Gary Wayne and Fritz Springmeier, thirteen bloodline families sit at the very top of the terrestrial command structure. But in the end, there is only one bloodline since all these royal thirteen families are related.

Other powerful families include the Algobrandini, Astor, Bundy, Giustiniani, Collins, DuPont, Freeman, Glucksberg, Rockefeller, Hohenzollern, Medici, Corsini, Wellesley, Odescalchi, Wurttemberg, Colonna, Wittelsbach, Del Banco, Bernadotte, Saxe-Coburg, Gothe, Warburg, Russell, Pallavacini, Hesse, Romanov, Van Duyn, Massimo, Savoy, and von Thurn und Taxis.

From the ranks of these families, a world monarch is selected. He presides over this Crown Council of 13. These are also the highest-ranking Freemasons in the world. Next, a Committee of 300 as described in former MI6 agent John Coleman's seminal book, *Conspirators' Hierarchy: The Story of the Committee of 300,* carries forth the agenda of the Crown Council of 13. The Committee of 300 is also made up strictly of bloodline family members.

The next one down the ladder is the Priory of Sion, which was founded in 1099 on Mt. Zion in the Kingdom of Jerusalem. A secret society founded by knight crusader Godfrey of Bouillon, its purpose was to spread the power of the Merovingian bloodline. The Priory of Sion is the hidden force behind Zionism since the plan is to crown a scion (grafted) bloodline fallen angel anti-Christ as world king in Jerusalem in order to cement their desired one world government and complete their Great Work of Ages. The Priory consists of only bloodline members.

Following them are the Rosicrucians, or Red Cross, which are bloodline family members charged with concealing and furthering the Zionist project to graft the Anunnaki bloodline onto humankind. They were a driving force behind the Invisible College, which became the Royal Society. The Rosicrucians are also charged with inverting the seven sacred sciences, as instructed by their Nephilim ancestors, in what is essentially a psychological warfare operation against humanity.

Next in line are the Royal Societies and Institutes that administer this inverted education through a vast array of fake science societies. These also work with the Anglican Church to control Protestant religious sects, which sprang from the Venetian bankers' funding of Martin Luther and the Reformation. The Royal Society sponsored the phony Enlightenment, along with Bacon, Hobbes, Malthus, Locke, Jung, Freud, and so on. Their job is to lie to humans as to the true nature of reality and our origins. Sadly, almost everything we think we know comes from these Satanists.

Chatham House hatches many of the most aggressive psychological operations through its Royal Institute of International Affairs, the British Broadcasting Corporation (BBC), and the Tavistock Institute, which is especially active in Hollywood movie production.

Below that are the secret society knights or operational arms. Many of these are intelligence assets. The Knights Templar, officially disbanded by the Catholic Church in 1307, have been absorbed into the Knights of Malta, who after an earlier religious split merged again with the Protestant Knights Hospitaller brethren to become the Sovereign Military Hospitaller Order of St. John of Jerusalem, of Rhodes, and of Malta. Nowadays, the Knights of Malta are charged with providing royal moles within the Vatican to keep tabs on the Pope.

Top-level Freemasons, Kabbalists, and Muslim Brotherhood agents run various global military, intelligence, political, and media wings. The City of London and the Bank of International Settlements in Basel, Switzerland, represent the corporate and banking arm of the bloodline. The Illuminati coordinates black operations including drug, arms, and human trafficking.

The Zionist project involves installing one of their scions, or "grafted ones", as a World Monarch on the throne in the Third Temple which the Rothschilds are currently building on the site of the stolen Al-Aqsa Mosque on the Temple Mount in Jerusalem.

This is near Mt. Zion where the Anunnaki hybrid Tribe of Dan, which became the Merovingian bloodline, originated. Israel sits at the center of a huge contiguous land mass that runs from Vladivostok to Windhoek and from Oslo to Singapore. This is why the region has always been highly strategic and volatile. This is also probably why the Anunnaki chose to land in the Sinai Peninsula, smack dab in the middle of the biggest chunk of dry land on planet earth.

But the crowning of this World King can, and will only, happen at the right time when conditions are conducive to such a massive coming-out by the royal bloodline. My guess is that it will follow a cataclysmic global war or economic collapse. A fearful public will be told of the Second Coming of Jesus, possibly on the heels of a fake alien invasion as envisioned in Project Blue Beam.

This king will actually be a Luciferian anti-Christ from one of the above-mentioned royal bloodlines in an attempt to bring in a Fourth Industrial Revolution via fifth-generation (5G) weaponized technology. Their utopian dream after this Great Reset is a New World Order based on the complete electronic enslavement of humanity.

The UK's Prince William is their current choice. And it is all about eugenics. William is not the son of King Charles III, who recently bragged of his lineage to Vlad the Impaler, otherwise known as Dracula. Rather, according to numerous Spanish and French media reports and books, William is the son of King Juan Carlos of Spain, with whom Diana had a eugenics-driven affair.

King Juan Carlos, who has lived in exile from Spain since his shady dealings with the Saudi Arabian monarchy were exposed in 2014, is from the House of Bourbon, which has ruled numerous European nations since its inception in 1268. Carlos has Merovingian, Bourbon, and Hapsburg roots while Diana came from the Spencer, Merovingian, and Plantagenet line.

Chapter 14

Neocolonialism

Crazy Horse was not just a battle-hardened warrior – he was also a visionary. How could he have known what he and his people were up against? The Lakota people could never in their wildest dreams have imagined that such wetiko insanity even existed in the world.

Other than a handful of tribes in the Amazon Basin and Borneo, the Plains Indians were among the last in the world to have contact with the wetiko Crown agents. Until the mid-19th century, they were living just as Wakan Tanka intended. The closest thing in their cosmology to evil was probably Iktomi, who appeared as a coyote and was known as a trickster. But even Iktomi the Trickster had positive qualities and became a helpful teacher when he pointed out erroneous behavior by playing tricks on misguided people.

The wetiko settlers and agents had been battered and bruised by the Crown for so long that their world view was almost just the opposite. To them, the world was full of evil. Danger lurked around every corner. The devil was on the loose and they had internalized his dark Luciferian Royal Society-orchestrated religion.

With the discovery of oil and advances in technology from three industrial revolutions in tow following WWII, the Crown set about to transform East India Company slavery and colonization into a new financial neocolonialism based, once again, on usury and debt.

Slaves had built up the infrastructure of the Crown in all corners of the world where their corporate tentacles operated. Ports, roads, water and sewer systems, plantations, and railroads had all been built by slavery. The heavy lifting was done, but the Crown had learned that slavery could be quite expensive.

So they set about to normalize a system where individuals and governments alike would be controlled through a new combination of wage slavery, financialization of the economy, and debt. Better to let the slaves transport and feed themselves and then tax the new wage slaves to relieve the burden of taxation on their Crown corporation cartels. In the early days of the United States it was the Crown corporation excise and import taxes that funded the entire US government.

Even before WWII had ended, the Crown pushed through the Bretton Woods Agreement of 1944. It represented the first agreement to govern monetary relations among different countries and included signatories from the United States, Canada, Western Europe, Japan, and Australia. It is instructive that it was signed before the US Air Force had even dropped the world's first nuclear bombs on Hiroshima and Nagasaki.

The agreement required countries to guarantee the convertibility of their currencies into US dollars. The International Monetary Fund (IMF) was launched to lend dollars to countries with balance of payments deficits. It also established the International Bank for Reconstruction and Development as part of a new World Bank Group. Both the World Bank and the IMF would be based in Washington, DC.

The World Bank would make leveraged loans to developing countries and the IMF would act as the enforcer to make sure those countries paid those loans back with interest. If they did not, the IMF was empowered to impose a list of austerity measures on the debtor nation, which always included the privatization of critical public infrastructure.

The City of London and Wall Street bankers represented by the World Bank and IMF, will often forgive debt in exchange for Crown corporation ownership of this privatized infrastructure. They call this a debt/equity swap. In 1995, the Warren Buffett-controlled Burlington Northern Railroad was handed almost the entire Mexican national rail system when banks led by Citigroup agreed to cancel Mexican debt owed to them.

Other forms of austerity include the formation of export processing zones, where Crown corporations can set up shop tax-free in the country in arrears, then process and ship their products from this zone, which is usually located at a Crown-controlled port. Sometimes the IMF demands that subsidies on basic food such as corn and tortillas are canceled. Government education, health care, and infrastructure spending can be ordered slashed. If the government is recalcitrant in carrying out these dictates, the country's currency will simply be devalued, plunging the population into hyperinflation and extreme poverty.

Meanwhile, the money lent from the World Bank tends to go towards "development" projects that benefit both the Crown contractors who do the construction and the Crown corporations who benefit from the completion of the project. World Bank money in the Philippines went to construct roads to ports near the Del Monte and Dole pineapple plantations.

A high percentage of these loans also end up going into the pockets of the local elite who mirror former British Raj stooges in India like the Tata and Birla families. These wealthy corrupt families then funnel their ill-gotten proceeds into City of London-controlled offshore banking centers, leaving impoverished locals on the hook to pay back the crushing debt created by this scam. This unpayable debt is then used as leverage by the royals to extract yet more resources and concessions from the newly "decolonized" country.

Every offshore banking center is officially sanctioned by and connected to the City of London, with only the Bank of England privy as to the exact ownership of numbered offshore accounts anywhere from the Cayman Islands to Bermuda to Vanuatu and the Isle of Jersey, just to name a few. Offshore banking is the main mechanism through which the royal bloodlines conceal the enormity of the wealth they have accumulated over the centuries.

Meanwhile, Chatham House was busy touting the wonders of "decolonization" as Pax Britannica gave way to "independent" nations headed by people who looked more like the local populations. Better to hide behind corrupt local politicians to keep real revolution against the Crown at bay and better to sell the plantations to a corrupt local elite through contract farming, since the farmer assumes all the risk.

In Africa, huge swaths of land were taken over by Crown charities such as the World Wildlife Fund under the pretense of "saving wildlife". Hunter-gatherers and subsistence farmers that lived within the boundaries of these new National Parks were simply told to leave. The same thing happened to the Blackfeet Indians in Montana when wilderness areas were established during the 1960s. And the same Crown "environmentalist" charities were involved in the theft of sacred areas like the Badger-Two Medicine.

After the Kennedy Assassination, which was orchestrated by the Crown, the bloodlines decided to hijack the environmental movement in order to occupy the growing number of "conspiracy theorists" – a term the CIA coined to discredit researchers who weren't buying the lone-gunman tale – with a new, bigger and ultimately unattainable cause.

The Kennedy hit was organized by Sir William Stephenson, an MI6 special agent who used a Crown agent corporation called Brinco as cover in planning the operation from the Tyndall Compound in Jamaica. Today Stephenson, whose nickname was Intrepid, is glorified as James Bond in a continuing series of Tavistock Institute Hollywood propaganda movies. Every time Americans watch a James Bond movie they are celebrating the assassin of one of the greatest American Presidents whose crime was standing up to Crown usury through his announcement that he would issue a silver-backed currency to compete with the Rothschild-controlled Federal Reserve. Talk about Satanic inversion.

Almost before the ink had dried on the Bretton Woods Agreement, countries from Indonesia to Kenya to India and Pakistan began to declare independence. Crown economists began to bandy about fancy new political jargon such as "comparative advantage" in order to steer these countries onto the path of export-led development, focusing on the production and export of one or two products where their nation held a supposed comparative advantage over other nations based on climate and resources.

A few sane economists warned that this strategy would leave these countries impoverished and permanently underdeveloped. They argued that these countries should focus instead on growing a diverse basic-needs economy that would provide for their residents.

But most went along with the Crown's IMF strategy of sucking the resources from the global South, leaving these countries under a pile of debt. The Ivory Coast was to commit to funding cocoa exports, Morocco should push out its sulfur, Jamaica its bauxite, and Namibia its diamonds. The Crown's multinationals would then process, ship, and market the finished product, adding value that could have gone to the impoverished nations instead. The record shows that these countries have remained underdeveloped, their sovereignty severely eroded by IMF debt restructuring mandates, and interest on the debt.

The US Agency for International Development (USAID) was deeply involved in what can only be seen as the intentional underdevelopment of the majority of the planet. Crown agent and former US Secretary of State, Henry Kissinger, openly talked about using food as a weapon. He is a neo-Malthusian obsessed with depopulation.

The typical pattern goes something like this: the World Bank loans money to a government, the money disappears quickly in a feeding frenzy of Crown contractors, corporations, and corrupt Freemason local elites, and the IMF makes its austerity demands.

From here it goes one of two ways. If the country complies with the IMF formula, it is sunk further into debt with a new World Bank loan, corruption becomes entrenched as Crown corporations take over the entire economy of the nation, and most of the country gets poorer.

If the country doesn't comply with the usury, their currency gets crushed by some Crown agent financier such as Rothschild lieutenant George Soros, prices go up, people revolt, and from time to time, armed revolutionaries take down the Crown's puppet regime.

The latter scenario is quite common, but you won't hear much about it on the Crown's television networks. The latest examples are Mali and Burkino Faso in West Africa. In 2022, both countries overthrew their corrupt French-backed puppet leaders, with the former country stating that French troops, who had come to Mali under the pretext of fighting ISIS terrorists, were actually backing the Islamic fundamentalists. But of course they were. It was the recent discovery of gold in Mali that had actually caused this so-called humanitarian intervention.

Throughout the period of this financial Bretton Woods neocolonialism there was a surge in Marxist revolutionary movements throughout Africa, Asia, and Central America. USAID would be sent into these conflict zones where they would deliver food bags and cans sporting the American flag to try and pacify the locals and endear them to the US and their local stooges.

The most infamous case of this was when fascist Guatemalan President, General Efrain Rios Mont, launched his "Beans for Rifles" program in Guatemala in the 1970s. This program, implemented by USAID, gave out food in Mayan villages in northern Guatemala in return for promises that these villages would not support the leftist Guerrilla Army of the Poor, which had taken up arms against the seven families who, to this day, control Guatemala.

If USAID fails to win the hearts and minds of the people the CIA gets into the game, organizing the economic hit men that John Perkins describes in his book of that title, and arming counter-revolutionaries to fight the rebels, as President Ronald Reagan did in Nicaragua in the 1980s, arming the contras to fight against Sandinista revolutionaries. Reagan did the same in El Salvador, Mozambique, Angola, and Namibia.

The resulting brush fire wars had the added benefit of depopulating these poor regions of the planet. It was much easier for Crown corporations to do business without having to deal with a large angry population. The best example of this today is the

Democratic Republic of the Congo, where over 5 million people have died over the past decade at the hands of local militias funded by Crown mining firms like Glencore.

The Congo contains most of the world's rare earth minerals, many of which are essential for the manufacturing of computers and smartphones. Ruled as a personal fiefdom by Saxe-Coburg Gotha and House of Orleans descendent King Leopold of Belgium until 1908, the country finally achieved independence in 1960. But it was short-lived. By 1961, revolutionary leader and newly-elected Prime Minister, Patrice Lumumba, was assassinated by US and Belgian-backed troops, paving the way for the 30-year dictatorship of Crown puppet Mobutu Sese Seko.

Sese Seko became a billionaire as he facilitated Crown hegemony over his country's many mineral deposits. On December 6, 2022, Crown-controlled Glencore was fined another $180 million by the Congolese government for corruption. Glencore was founded by Crown fugitive financier Marc Rich, whom Rhodes Scholar turned President Bill Clinton pardoned as he was leaving office. Based in Baar, Switzerland and the City of London in 2013, Glencore merged with Xstrata to become the world's largest commodity trader. It handles 3% of the world's oil consumption and has more ships than the British Navy.

Chapter 15

Crown Deception Becomes Public Perception

The entire process of "decolonization" took the deception, through which the royal bloodline has always concealed its power, to a whole different level. Hiding behind black and brown-skinned African, Asian, and Latin American governments, the City of London bankers sank the global South into an unpayable sea of debt. Meanwhile, the Temple Bar hatched a freehold land ownership system that displaced millions more hunting and gathering people, while magically landing all mines, timber, oilfields, and arable land into the hands of Crown corporations.

Propaganda was always an important tool in the Crown arsenal. But with the development of their media and intelligence arms in the 20th century, deception became increasingly important in forming public perception. The reality was that these media and intelligence wings had been joined at the hip from the very beginning.

In 1909, on the heels of forming the Business Round Table to silently perpetuate the British Empire, a secret society of the Crown known as the Pilgrims Society organized A Parliament of the Press: The First Imperial Press Conference, out was which was formed the Empire Press Union.

The Pilgrims Society was founded by Viscount Alfred Milner and Cecil Rhodes, the very same people who convened the Business Round Table. Other founding Pilgrims included C. Arthur Pearson, Earl Arthur James Balfour, and General Lord Earl Roberts.

On June 29, 1909, British Prime Minister Herbert Asquith 1st Earl of Oxford and Asquith formed two subcommittees under the Committee of Imperial Defence, known as the Colonial Defence and the Home Defence. These were to be part of a new Secret Service Bureau and would eventually be known as MI-6 and MI-5, respectively. These new spy agencies would report only to the Prime Minister and would be staffed by newspapermen from the Empire Press Union.

In 1926, King-Emperor George V of the House of Windsor and Saxe-Coburg Gotha hosted the First Imperial Conference. The emperor title had been added to the bloodline title after the East India Company ceded control of the British Raj in India to the British Crown in 1858. It was at this First Imperial Conference that Pilgrims Society founder and Lord President of the Privy Council, Alfred Balfour, announced his Balfour Declaration, which he had earlier written as a personal letter to Lord Walter Rothschild, seeking his rubber stamp.

Interestingly, the Balfour Declaration is remembered mostly for laying the groundwork for the creation of Israel out of what was British Palestine. More importantly, and less known, is that it also created the British Commonwealth of Nations from the former territories of Pax Britannica. The fact that Balfour was Lord President of the Privy Council informs us that the Business Round Table, Pilgrims Society, Empire Press Union, MI-6, MI-5, and the Commonwealth were all part of a deceptive "decolonization" plan hatched at Buckingham Palace.

The latter would serve as the template for the post WWII fake decolonization that was to come. But first, the Crown would need tighter control over its transatlantic military gendarme United States Corporation. They would need to ensure senior partner status in this new "special relationship" through control of US intelligence operations.

On August 14, 1941, less than four months before the Pearl Harbor false flag that drug the United States Corporation into WWII, the Five Eyes Alliance was born as part of the Atlantic Charter. In 1943, the US and Britain signed the BRUSA Agreement, facilitating cooperation between the US Department of War and the British Code and Cypher School.

Following WW II, US Army Chief of Staff George Marshall, at the insistence of the British, agreed to share intelligence with Australia, New Zealand, Canada, and the UK. In 1946, the year after the war ended, Britain's Government Code and Cypher School was renamed Government Communications Headquarters or GCHQ. One year later in 1947, the US Central Intelligence Agency was formed. In 1952, the National Security Agency was founded. And in 1961, the Defense Intelligence Agency was formed. The FBI and the National Geo-Spatial Intelligence Agency would also become part of the Crown's Five Eyes intelligence apparatus.

Crown control over these well-coordinated and intertwined intelligence agencies gave the City of London Corporation and its many global tentacles the ability to infiltrate and control newly "decolonized" governments. Just as they had learned to hide behind local straw man governments – and just as Dole had learned to contract out its farming operations to the local elite in the Philippines – the Crown also increasingly controlled the global South nations through a system of government contracts.

These contracts could come through a local government via a World Bank loan, or through a Western government under the auspices of "aid". The Crown's corporations also came to control contracts with Western governments to administer a wide range of government agencies for them. Contract law has always been an obsession of the lizard brain. It provides the framework for British Maritime Law, or Law of the Sea – a formula hatched and carried out worldwide by the City of London's Temple Bar.

The Five Eyes intelligence agencies took the deception one step further as they learned to contract out the training of right-wing paramilitary groups to put down leftist worker rebellions and governments alike in the "decolonized" countries. Israeli and Taiwanese intelligence agencies became quick favorites. These rebellions occurred everywhere that Crown multinationals pillaged the resources of a country.

In Guatemala, it was the United Fruit Company, where workers rose up on its plantations and elected leftist Jacobo Arbenz as president of the country. By 1954, the CIA had organized a coup to depose him.

A year earlier in 1953, the CIA and MI-6 overthrew the Iranian government of Mohammed Mosssadegh after he threatened to nationalize the Crown's British Petroleum interests. In 1973, leftist Chilean President Salvador Allende was overthrown by Crown-agent and Rockefeller lieutenant Henry Kissinger and the CIA. General Augusto Pinochet was installed as a dictator to protect Rockefeller's Anaconda Copper interests.

The CIA's greatest hits list is long and continues apace to this day. In 2009, the CIA ousted leftist Honduran President Manuel Zelaya in a coup. In 2013, they poisoned socialist Venezuelan President Hugo Chavez, whose country sits on the Western Hemisphere's largest oil deposits. One year later in 2014, they orchestrated the incident on Kiev's Maidan Square that led to the ouster of pro-Russian and democratically-elected President Victor Yanukovych.

In 2019, the CIA forced Bolivian President Evo Morales to resign after his Movement for Socialism Party threatened Crown natural gas interests. And in 2022, they ousted leftist Peruvian President Pedro Castillo after his Minister of Foreign Affairs Hector Bejar announced that Peru would no longer go along with US-led sanctions aimed at Venezuela. Bejar proclaimed that it was the CIA that had created the "far-left" Shining Path in Peru in the 1980s in order to counter the genuinely leftist Tupac Amaru Revolutionary Movement.

Deception is the very basis of intelligence work and recently, with help from the Open Society Foundation – run first by George Soros and currently by Lord Mark Malloch Brown – their tactics have become even more deceiving. Working closely with the National Endowment for Democracy and other Crown-funded NGO contractors, the CIA learned to market their interventions with names like Arab Spring (Tunisia and Egypt), the Rose Revolution

(Georgia), the Cedar Revolution (Lebanon), and the Orange Revolution (Ukraine).

Lord Mark Malloch-Brown's previous position was as Chairman of the Board of Smartmatic, the world's largest voting technology firm. He also chaired the Royal African Society. The Toronto-based Dominion Voting Systems is also controlled by the Crown through Commonwealth henchmen in Canada. Both companies came under scrutiny after the 2020 US Presidential elections. Had Crown trickery and deception reached a level where they were actually electronically-rigging voting machines worldwide?

Soros is a long-time Rothschild lieutenant, who manages the Crown's offshore investments. The Quantum NV fund based in Curacao is one of the most important of these. Both Soros and Malloch-Brown are leaders of the World Economic Forum, led by Klaus Schwab, who recently received the Spear of Destiny from the Habsburgs. This is the vehicle through which the Crown promotes its trans-humanist Fourth Industrial Revolution and The Great Reset.

But at the apex of the Crown's deception are their subsidiary media outlets. These "mediums" or "channels" are designed to send out a "newscast" that consists of a pack of convoluted lies designed to keep the viewer in a sort of trance, with the emphasis on cultivating a the dark view of human nature and support for the demonic Crown system.

When CIA Director William Colby was questioned by the Church Committee in 1974 as to extent of Operation Mockingbird – a program through which the CIA infiltrated major media corporations – he replied, "That is something we will have to look at in closed session". The number of media personalities who are on the CIA payroll is far greater than we think.

In the best-case scenario, these news "anchors" are simply handed a script to read from the Associated Press, which in turn gets its wire stories from the intelligence agencies. The Crown's Tavistock Institute for Human Behavior has been crucial in the Privy Council's understanding of how certain stories and ways of delivering or "spinning" them affects the general population.

Both intelligence and media assets are recruited from bloodline families and their secret societies. CNN anchor Anderson Cooper, for example, hales from the Vanderbilt family. NBC is part of the Crown agent General Electric conglomerate. CBS is controlled by Crown agent Westinghouse Corporation, which controls a big chunk of the UK Nuclear Weapons establishment along with Lockheed Martin and SERCO. Fox News is owned by Zionist Rupert Murdoch and Saudi Crown Prince Alaweed bin Talal. CNN is owned by the Crown's Atlantic Telephone & Telegraph, which you know as AT&T. And ABC is run by the Disney Corporation.

The US Council on Foreign Relations – a subsidiary of the Chatham House-based Royal Institute of International Affairs – is a major recruiting ground for media, intelligence, and banking assets. Sons and daughters of high-ranking Freemasons are recruited in this way, as are members of Oxford, Cambridge, Harvard, and Yale fraternities and secret societies.

In summation, what the royal Anunnaki bloodline had learned was, as Hitler propaganda minister Josef Mengele said, "The bigger the lie, the easier it is to convince people that it is true." He also said, "The more we do to you, the less you seem to think we are doing it."

By refining the propaganda and repeating it more forcefully and more often, the Crown would be able to dial down the overwhelming military force and outright slavery, focusing instead on the hearts and minds of the people. The advent of television, which interestingly coincided with a bad round of "Asian flu" across America, along with a series of cybernetic studies culminating in the infamous CIA MK-Ultra program, paved the way for the next frontier of fifth generation (5G) weaponry capable of targeting individuals, groups, and entire populations with mind controlling radio frequencies.

Chapter 16

The Royal Alchemist Assault on Humanity

Not content with this quiet consolidation of global Crown power, the CIA launched their aptly named Project Monarch in the early 1960's. The Crown and its CIA agents were looking for methods of mind control that involved various chemical agents that had become available as the Crown's oil companies discovered new alchemistic techniques to permeate the entire global economy in derivatives of their black gold.

MK-Ultra was at the center of Project Monarch from which sprang offshoots like Spellbinder, which sought to create mind-controlled assassins, and Operation Often, which explored black magic and the occult. These experiments attempted to put subjects into what they termed "marionette syndrome", modifying their thoughts and behaviors to put them into a puppet-like state through which they could be manipulated by their CIA handlers.

These controlled stimulus response sequences were termed "imperial conditioning" by the researchers. Satanic rituals were used to enhance the trauma experienced by the usually drugged subjects. LSD became the CIA's drug of choice.

As opposition to the Vietnam War gained momentum in the US the Crown's social engineers used Billy Mellon Hitchcock of the Mellon banking family to spread LSD throughout the West Coast protest movement through his Brotherhood of Eternal Love. Soon militant protests were overshadowed by images of hippie street urchins in San Francisco's Haight-Ashbury district. This Tavistock Institute project created the desired cultural backlash, sinking anti-war presidential candidates Eugene McCarthy and George McGovern in favor of Richard Nixon.

This was hardly the first pharmacological trick utilized by the Crown. In 1910, the Flexner Report had already laid the groundwork for modern medicine coming under control of the newly formed Rockefeller Foundation. In 1905, the Rockefellers began to steer the US education system into subservience towards his Crown patrons when he founded his General Education Board to "advise" public education. Now he would use the Flexner Report to steer public health policy in a direction which would benefit his Standard Oil Trust.

The Rockefellers were also at the forefront of the eugenics movement, which seeks to eliminate undesirable bloodlines. To this end they funded fellow racist Margaret Sanger, who founded the nation's first birth control clinic in Brooklyn in 1916. By 1921, Sanger had founded the American Birth Control League, which in 1942, became Planned Parenthood.

Though in high demand as a speaker at Ku Klux Klan rallies during her tenure, Sanger is today revered like a saint by supposed progressives. Her writings tell the real story. In a 1939 letter to Dr. Clarence Gamble, Sanger wrote, "We don't want the word to go out that we want to exterminate the Negro population".

Most Planned Parenthood abortion clinics are indeed located in black neighborhoods. In a paper she wrote in 1932 titled, *My Way to Peace*, Sanger urged, "Apply a stern and rigid policy of sterilization and segregation to that grade of population whose progeny is tainted, or whose inheritance is such that objectionable traits may be transmitted to offspring."

In another paper written in 1918, *Morality and Birth Control*, Sanger railed, "All of our problems are the result of over-breeding among the working class... Knowledge of birth control is essentially moral. Its general, though prudent, practice must lead to a higher individuality and ultimately to a cleaner race."

But Sanger and her eugenics high rollers were just the tip of the iceberg when it came to the Crown's weaponization of the medicine establishment. Abraham Flexner is known as the founder of modern medical education. After his 1910 report drew the attention of the Carnegie's and the Rockefeller's, his brother Simon became a researcher at the Rockefeller Institute for Medical Research.

Later, this institution would be renamed Rockefeller University and would eventually lay the groundwork for standardized pharmacological and surgical-based Western medicine. Doctors would now prescribe new alchemical poisons called "prescription drugs", which would be manufactured by Crown-controlled pharmaceutical firms. These consisted of oil-based synthetics from the Standard Oil Trust combined with ancient medicinal plants stolen from their rightful hunting and gathering stewards in all corners of the planet.

So-called "alternative" medical practitioners were discredited, though they based their practices on much older and more rigorously tested methods. Herbal medicine, which had been practiced for at least 100,000 years, was suddenly under Crown assault, even though they were using the exact same herbs in their new "magic elixirs".

Simultaneously, hemp came under attack. Even though King James I had ordered every colonist to "grow 100 hemp plants" in order to contribute to fiber production in the New World, the plant now competed with Rockefeller's International Paper Company and DuPont's oil-based nylon. By 1923, Canada had banned hemp altogether and by the mid-1930's, the US regulated marijuana. The 1970 Controlled Substances Act officially outlawed cannabis, even for medical purposes.

With the medical establishment now weaponized under Crown control, the royal bloodlines launched an alchemists war on planet earth using their medical wing as cover. Water, air and food were targeted with a slew of new chemicals concocted by Crown firms like Monsanto, Dow, and BASF. IBM manufactured what are now called "forever chemicals" and inserted them into personal care and cleaning products. These chemicals stay in people's bodies forever, slowly making them sick.

DDT and paraquat were sprayed generously on California fruits and vegetables. Some researchers connect this to the polio outbreak in the US in the early 1950s. Instead of looking into this, the Rockefeller medicine show funded Dr. Jonas Salk who concocted a deadly polio vaccine, which we now know is responsible for an epidemic of brain cancers in men born before 1964 who got this poisonous injection.

While the Crown's American Medical Association told the public there were deadly viruses inside our frail human bodies that would make us sick if we didn't get their cartel-produced vaccines, the Crown's chemical wing was busy poisoning Americans. Virus means "venom" in Latin. And coronavirus in Latin translates "Crown venom".

Germ theory was first put forward by Venetian Girolamo Fracastoro, who has a crater on the moon named after him. It took off in the 1850's with the work of Louis Pasteur. Pasteur graduated from the Royal College at Besancon in 1839. He was a member of the Royal Society and recipient of the Legion of Honor Grand Cross. He received the Albert Medal from the Royal Society of the Arts in 1882 and the Leeuwenhoek Medal from the Royal Netherlands Academy of Arts & Sciences in 1895.

Pasteur's Crown-funded research was expanded by Robert Koch, who became a director at the Royal Prussian Institute for Infectious Diseases in 1891. The two are held up as the fathers of microbiology. Prior to the Crown's proclamation that germ theory would guide their new oil-based medicine, the common explanation for diseases was miasma theory or terrain theory, which maintains that disease is caused by exposure to environmental toxins.

The repercussions of this new medical paradigm were far-reaching. Instead of funding clean water and sewer systems in the global South, postwar USAID and NGO medical crusaders launder their charitable contributions into massive vaccination campaigns that are killing and sterilizing people.

But the ruling class know full well what they are doing. Their goal is not a healthy human population. Their goal is depopulation. Technology pirate turned vaccine expert Bill Gates, whose father once headed Planned Parenthood, enunciated this in a 2010 Ted Talk in which he said, "The world today has 6.8 billion people. That's headed up to about nine billion. Now, if we do a really great job on new vaccines, health care, reproductive health services, we could lower that by perhaps 10 or 15 percent."

The Anunnaki Crown forced humanity into agriculture and then herded them into dirty crowded cities after stealing their "freehold" land. Now they cranked up their noxious smokestack factories, often locating them on rivers, which they used to dump their poisonous chemical concoctions into. What better way to deflect attention from these crimes against humanity than to declare germ theory as medical truth, while denying funding for studies into the toxicity of your new arsenal of poisons? In 1945, Grand Rapids, Michigan, became the first city to fluoridate its public drinking water.

In 1970, Monsanto scientist John E. Franz discovered glyphosate, which would become known worldwide as Roundup. Ponder that word for a minute. A decade later, a massive farm crisis sent shock waves through the American heartland as small farms were foreclosed upon en masse by the Crown's banks and their land taken over by a few wealthy farmers in each local area.

The problem was that these wealthy farmers were also deeply in debt to the same banks. And as part of their loan requirements, the agribusiness operators were required to spray Roundup on their fields to improve yields, which in turn would drive grain prices down, ensuring a cheap supply of corn and soybeans to bloodline grain merchants such as Cargill and Bunge. Much of this grain was then fed to cattle in western Kansas feedlots that were owned by the same vertically integrated grain giants.

The glyphosate in Roundup mimics glycine, one of our body's most important amino acids. Today, our entire food supply is tainted with glyphosate so the glycine receptors in our bodies are choked with a pseudo-glycine that prevents us from building collagen and key proteins that the human body and mind needs in order to be healthy. The result has been a rash of gut and nervous system related diseases, mental health disorders, and an epidemic of heart disease and stroke – all of which are controlled with natural glycine.

In the 1960s, the Rockefeller Foundation had funded the much-touted Green Revolution, through which they forced genetically modified (GMO) seeds on farmers from Mexico to the Philippines. These seeds were eventually bred to be resistant to Roundup. And by 2015, 89% of corn, 94% of soybeans and 89% of cotton grown in the US were GMO strains.

This combination of glyphosates and GMO Frankenfoods continues to wreak havoc on the health of the global population, which in turn translates into huge profits for the medical industrial complex. In typical parasite fashion, the Crown's law firms are now cashing in as thousands of class action lawsuits linking Roundup to numerous types of cancer play out. Meanwhile, Monsanto has become part of Bayer, which has its roots in the Nazi IG Farben chemical cartel.

But the invention of wireless fidelity, or wifi, is where the Crown really hit the modern-day jackpot. Not only could they use the phones and computers that operate on wifi to mind control and enslave their subjects in a new type of electronic feudalism, they could also use the lethal radio frequencies used for wifi to quietly carry out a mass depopulation program. Wifi operates at 2.4 gigahertz, the exact same frequency that the body utilizes to process water molecules. Again, our bodies can't distinguish between the two and people are being severely dehydrated and sickened as a result.

With their Fourth Industrial Revolution underway, and under the cover of global COVID lockdowns, the Crown greatly expanded its network of 5G cell towers. In the Western world, most of them were erected by Crown Castle Corporation, which has now changed its name to Aqiba and is headquartered on Fleet Street in the City of London. Researched and refined at the Department of Defense's Lawrence Livermore Laboratories in the late 1960s, 5G is a weapons system.

This system has the ability to operate at 60 gigahertz, which is the exact same frequency that our bodies use to take up oxygen via the hemoglobin in our blood. Our bodies get confused and pretty soon, we can't breathe. Interestingly, this was the main symptom of "COVID-19" patients.

Having already declared war on food, water, and air, the Crown decided to declare war on life itself through its current crusade against carbon, which it tells us causes "climate change", while its mouthpieces like Al Gore and its owners like King Charles continue to jet around the planet. These private jets emit more carbon emissions in one day than a car does in two years. Carbon is the building block for all of life on this planet, so why would we need less of it, unless of course we wanted to end all life here?

Meanwhile, animal populations across the world have dropped 70% in the last fifty years. Many areas of the world are reporting that the insects that once lived there are completely gone. US life expectancy has dropped for two consecutive years. Male sperm counts are plummeting. Female miscarriages are skyrocketing.

But rather than deal with the issues caused by poisons manufactured by corporate tentacles, the climate criminals invert the conversation and parasitically hide behind a Swedish teenage girl named Greta Thunberg. And while Goldman Sachs and BlackRock financialize the climate scare via ESG scores and trading of carbon credits, the glitterati amuse themselves jetting off to Davos to discuss new methodologies that ensure our further enslavement.

Chapter 17

The Bloodline Take Down of America: Part II

The Eurodollar market began in the early 1960s when Eastern European pro-Soviet governments wanted to be able to hold US dollar accounts at Western European banks. But it really exploded in the 1980s when President Ronald Reagan's deregulation frenzy allowed US corporations to hold their assets in overseas Eurodollar accounts. This disappeared into the even less regulated City of London/Bank of England-controlled offshore banking network, amidst a swirl of oil, guns, and drug money.

During the Bush and Clinton years the bloodline made yet more progress in bringing their American military gendarme to heel. The Bush family are blood relatives to the Windsor clan that currently occupies Buckingham Palace. Clinton, who some researchers believe is the illegitimate son of former Arkansas Governor Winthrop Rockefeller, was a Rhodes Scholar.

Clinton's now-deceased patron, Cecil Rhodes, had written that the aim of his last will and testament was, "to establish a trust, to and for the establishment and promotion and development of a secret society, the true aim and object whereof shall be the extension of British rule throughout the world...and the ultimate recovery of the United States of America as an integral part of the British Empire."

Clinton and the Bushes further deregulated the Crown's cartels. Many corporations, having already stashed their Eurodollars in City of London offshore tax havens like Panama and Bermuda, now used those havens to dodge corporate taxes, robbing the United States of much needed revenue that it needed to upgrade its decaying infrastructure.

Clinton repealed the Glass-Steagal Act, which had been put into place following the Great Depression after Congressional hearings had revealed that Goldman Sachs and the other Crown banks had caused it. It separated commercial banking from investment banking.

The Bushes pushed laws making bankruptcy more difficult for the average person while exempting pharmaceutical firms from liability for vaccine injuries and allowing telecommunications giants to plow forward with their deadly 5G agenda. Both came to the rescue of British Petroleum when their oil interests in Iraq were threatened.

These three Crown agent Presidents passed a slew of "free trade agreements" that allowed the cartels to set up more manufacturing companies in countries with cheap labor. These included the General Agreement on Trade and Tariffs (GATT), the North American Free Trade Agreement (NAFTA), and the Central American Free Trade Agreement (CAFTA).

These corporate windfall deals were to be arbitrated by an overarching World Trade Organization (WTO), which was well-staffed with cartel CEOs. Its current Director-General, Ngozi Okonjo-Iweala, was Chairman of the Board for the Bill Gates-funded Global Vaccine Alliance (GAVI). She was also a director at the old opium laundry Standard Chartered PLC and was the Crown's censorship lynch pin at Twitter.

It was during this time that the Crown's deindustrialization takedown of their United States Corporation military gendarme reached its crescendo. Key to the new silent Pax Britannica was to limit the power of any particular national government. When German engineering threatened Crown hegemony, the Crown marched out WWI and WWII to knock the German economy down. Now they wanted to use this same tactic to limit the power of the US government.

The lizard brain operates under contract law and it was during the Bush I and II and Clinton administrations that a swarm of

Crown-controlled contractors got their talons into a shrinking US government that was privatizing even its military. British Prime Minister, Tony Blair, passed laws granting the City of London yet more power. The biggest of these City contractors is SERCO.

In 1999, HP scientist Richard P. Walker was granted a patent for what would become known as the internet of everything, now better known as 5G. Walker and the rest of his Silicon Valley colleagues had been fed military technology by Crown corporations Lockheed Martin and IBM.

HP spun off Agilent Technologies that same year as the vehicle through which the Walker patent would come to fruition. All ensuing patents pertaining to 5G would be mysteriously absorbed by Agilent, whether in the areas of surveillance, cybernetics, genetic engineering, human micro-chipping, or "wet works".

The corporation pushing Walker's Agilent patent forward is SERCO, a powerful British company close to Lockheed Martin, Westinghouse, General Electric, and British Aerospace (BAE). The first and last are the two biggest defense contractors in the world. The middle two own CBS and NBC. All four are part of Crown Agents, USA Inc. The golden share in all of these companies was historically controlled through British Nuclear Fuels (BNFL) by Queen Elizabeth II.

In 2009, BNFL was shut down after spinning off its Westinghouse subsidiary. They had acquired Westinghouse in 1999, four years after Westinghouse bought CBS. BNFL's nuclear plants had been privatized in 1996 and were taken over by British Energy. The same year BNFL shut down, British Energy was taken over by Electricite de France.

In 2000, SERCO and Lockheed Martin took control of the UK's Aldermaster weapons site. They also control two-thirds of the British Atomic Weapons Establishment (AWE). The other third was owned by BNFL. During the past decade, AWE began exporting stolen US-enriched uranium from a Eunice, New Mexico, facility through its URINCO subsidiary. They were aided in this effort by the Highland Group, whose members include the Clintons and former FBI Director, Robert Mueller, who would later play a key role in the phony Russiagate allegations.

SERCO controls immigration and owns a pathology lab in the UK and runs detention centers, prisons and hospitals in Australia and New Zealand. But the bulk of its income comes from no-bid US government contracts granted to it by members of Senior Executive Services (SES). SES consists of government insiders who, unlike a typical civil servant, cannot be fired after one year of service. President Obama appointed 8,000 of these Crown agents.

SERCO receives $15-20 billion dollars a year in US government contracts. It runs 63 air traffic control towers, manages Obama Care, runs city parking meters and lots, as well as buses and trains, overseas Overseas Private Investment Corporation (OPIC) loans, and handles all USAID shipments.

But 75% of SERCO's contracts are with the Department of Defense. With offices in the Bank of England-controlled offshore dirty money banking centers of Guernsey, Jersey, and the Cayman Islands, SERCO runs "security" for all branches of the US military and our intelligence services.

SERCO is deeply involved in the US Space Program through Aerospace Corporation, which plans to deploy 24,000 new 5G-enabling satellites via Elon Musk's SpaceX and Amazon's OneWeb in the next few years. SERCO also holds contracts with Bill Gates' Millennium Foundation involving the sterilization of Africans and Indians through vaccinations.

Founded in 1929, SERCO came out of RCA, another Crown corporation which morphed mostly into GE. RCA is best known for its consumer electronics, but its main business had been military radar and sonar equipment. It is this same technology which is now being deployed as 5G. In my book, *Big Oil & Their Bankers...*, I pinpoint RCA as a key player in the Crown assassination of President John F. Kennedy via Chairman David Sarnoff.

During the early 1960s, RCA developed the UK Ballistic Missile Early Warning System. During the 1980s, they were awarded the contract to support the new European Space Agency and began maintaining London's street lights. In 1987, with much of RCA absorbed into GE, what remained became SERCO.

During the 1990s SERCO took its services international, focusing on the Five Eyes Alliance countries of the UK, Canada, Australia, New Zealand, and the US. The middle three countries are part of the Commonwealth and thus controlled directly by the British Crown. SERCO also began operating in the Crown's puppet Gulf Cooperation Council (GCC) monarchies in the Middle East where it runs all air traffic control operations. It also gained control of Iraq's Civil Aviation Authority. This makes Crown drug, arms, oil, and human smuggling in and out of its new Dubai hub a breeze.

SERCO provides technical support for CERN's particle accelerator, manages transport services at North District Hospital in Hong Kong (another major drug trafficking center), and provides support for military bases in the Five Eyes nations. It manages the UK National Physics Laboratory and trains soldiers in the US and Germany.

SERCO dominates contracts from US Homeland Security and is in charge of FEMA Region 9, which includes Alaska, Hawaii, and the US West Coast – all of which have recently experienced a slew of "natural" disasters.

SERCO began providing IT support for European Parliament in 2014, began training US firefighters in Afghanistan in 2016, and began operating European Meteorological Satellites in 2017.

SERCO specializes in handling sensitive cyberdata, including criminal records, driver's license records, vaccination records, DNA databases, and military records and communications. Big Data is the new Big Oil and SERCO was now in the catbird's seat when came to using this data to control the Five Eyes governments and their citizens.

But SERCO's most important GCHQ infiltration came in 2015 when it was awarded the patent classification contract in the US, essentially commandeering the US Patent Office. In this capacity, they are able to steer and manage the Walker 5G patent in the Crown's desired weaponized direction. That direction, according to the CIA's own Deagel Report, is towards a 70% reduction in both US and UK populations by 2025.

SERCO is run by two British Knights Hospitallers. Sir Roy Gardner is SERCO's Chairman who handles, according to their own website, "relations with the City (of London) and major stakeholders (Queen Elizabeth II)". CEO Rupert Soames is Winston Churchill's grandson. In 2010, he was awarded Officer of the Order of the British Empire. Both came from Crown Agent General Electric, which manufactures both the smart meters and the new LED lighting being rolled out to facilitate the Crown's new 5G mind control weapons system.

With this "silent weapon for quiet wars" now at their disposal, the Crown seeks to achieve full spectrum dominance over the planet's humans. Their Satanic Babylonian coming-out party could now take place. Firmly in the driver's seat with Crown cartel control over every facet of life, they could begin to tell us exactly who they are – Anunnaki invaders.

Chapter 18

The Internet/Social Media Reveal

Modern computers were first developed by the IBM Corporation, using Nazi scientists smuggled into the US via Operation Paperclip. Computers were introduced to the general public during the 1980s, but the Crown's military, banking, and intelligence organizations had been using them for three decades. Cisco was known as the NSA's "golden child", while Intel created back-door microchips that allowed NSA access to all computers.

In 1966, the director of the US Defense Department's Advanced Research Projects Agency's (ARPA) Information Processing Techniques Office, Bob Taylor, initiated the project that would lead to what we now call the internet. Additional research was done at the Stanford Research Institute and at UK's National Physical Laboratory (NPL), whose operation was contracted out to SERCO in 1995. This occurred simultaneously with the release of the internet to the general public.

ARPA became DARPA (Defense Advanced Research Projects Agency) and by 1970, it had set about assigning IP addresses and selling domain names to the inevitable tech monopolies that would follow. Originally, the internet was used by the National Security Agency for its signals intelligence operations. In other words, it was used as a means to deliver disinformation and propaganda to enemies of the Crown.

In 1995, the Defense Communications Agency took control of the internet. This coincided with SERCO's new NPL contract and with the release of the internet to the public. Now the propaganda arm of the US military and SERCO would preside over a misinformation explosion that the planet had never seen, giving a whole new meaning to the phrase "computer programmer", whose bread was buttered giving "commands".

With the internet cast, the World Wide Web was spun as a means to trap individuals whose opinions did not line up with the agenda of the Crown. Now DARPA would set about developing the two mechanisms, which would be used to spring the internet trap – social media and search engines.

In 2004, DARPA quietly shelved its LifeLog project, which *Wired Magazine* once called, "an ambitious effort to build a database tracking a person's entire existence". On the very same day that DARPA shut LifeLog down, Mark Zuckerberg announced the launch of Facebook. Most of Facebook's initial investment came from In-Q-Tel, the investment arm of the CIA. Using the typical Crown methodology, the Crown's intelligence agencies had simply contracted out a critical Tavistock-developed psychological warfare operation to Facebook, which would sell this voluntary personal information dump to the public as "social media".

DARPA now dedicated more resources to a project that it called Mimix. They funneled money into the Stanford Research Institute, which had become the US military's computer research hub shortly after WWII and eventually spawned Silicon Valley. The DARPA Mimix project was eventually contracted out to Google. The name "Mimix" is instructive of the goal of DARPA's Google project to create a hive mind consensus from the global population, who would increasingly "mimic" what a Google search told them was gospel truth. DARPA refers to this as "birds of a feather". The goal is to create a "singularity" where all humans mimic Crown propaganda and behavior, eliminating all opposition to their Luciferian ideology.

Google's parent company is Alphabet, which also controls YouTube. The name is certainly interesting since the rise of the internet and social media is akin to the Tower of Babel legend, where the alphabet was scrambled by a new group of Semitic language speakers who suddenly appeared on the scene. Was it now the job of "Alphabet" to repeat this Anunnaki project to shut down communication and debate and replace it with senseless babble that would allow their hegemony to remain unopposed?

A language learning company called Babbel was launched in 2008. And in late 2022, a new movie was released starring Brad Pitt called Babylon. The introduction of television was a boon to the Crown's propaganda efforts. Now they would trap humans into an internet where they became willing, but unwitting participants in the demise of their privacy and critical faculties.

Television is a one-way information stream, but the internet is interactive. Social media adds peer pressure to the equation. Most people succumb to it and cave into the hive mind singularity consensus to avoid conflict. Those who question this increasingly Satanic consensus are isolated and harassed. The most intelligent of these are banned from the various CIA contractor social media platforms.

On February 16, 2019, at the Munich Security Conference, Google delivered a 30-page white paper outlining their strategy for combating "fake news" on their various internet platforms, including YouTube. Fake news would come to refer to any information that disagreed with the Crown's agenda.

Their Orwellian proposals included "giving people context about the information they see", "making authoritative sources readily available" and preventing YouTube uploads of "bizarre conspiracy theories".

Google partners in this effort include the First Draft Coalition, the Trust Project, and the International Fact-Checking Network. All are front groups for the mainstream media organizations and NGOs run by the global elite.

One of the major players in this internet censorship is Haymarket Media Group, a London-based Royal Society tentacle led by former Thatcher cabinet minister Michael Heseltine.

Haymarket has its headquarters in Bridge House, home to Bridge House Estates, a charitable trust founded by Royal charter in

1282 by the City of London Corporation. Bridge House makes its grants through the City Bridge Fund, which along with City's Cash and City Fund, are the three funds managed by the City of London Corporation.

Interestingly, the United States Federal Bridge Certification Authority (FBCA) is the basis for secure US intergovernmental communications. Many of these communications are contracted and administered by Crown Agent SERCO. Is FBCA being monitored by the City Bridge Fund or Bridge House Estates?

Haymarket Media Group founded the Trust Project, which places a "trust mark" on websites that it deems reliable. Other Trust Project founders included *The Globe & Mail*, Hearst Television, *The Washington Post*, and *Economist* magazine. The *Economist* is 21%-owned by the Rothschilds. Other *Economist* owners include the Cadbury and Schroder families which bankrolled Hitler, the Agnelli family, the Lazard family, and Baron Layton.

The First Draft Coalition is also based in London. Partners include CNN, BBC, ABC News, Facebook, *The Telegraph*, and *The Washington Post*. Funding comes from the Google News Initiative, Rothschild-lieutenant George Soros' Open Society Foundation, the Ford Foundation, the Koch Brothers, and the Bill & Melinda Gates Foundation.

First Draft specifically targets "conspiracy communities". Their website talks of the need to "inoculate" against, "conspiracies about global networks of power", further stating that, "debunking or explaining these conspiracies…gives them not only legitimacy but a set of keywords for your audience to use to search for more information… Before the internet, such remote communities struggled to connect because it was so difficult to meet face to face. Now such communities can flourish."

The third Google censorship partner is the International Fact-Checking Coalition, which is operated by the Poynter Institute. Major funders of Poynter include Andrew W. Mellon Foundation, Charles Koch Foundation, National Endowment for Democracy, and Soros and Lord Mark Malloch-Brown's colored revolution-plotting Open Society Foundation.

In 1964, a year after the Crown's MI-6 special agent, Sir William Stephenson, assassinated President John F. Kennedy, the CIA worried that many Americans were not buying the Oswald lone-gunmen theory and coined the term "conspiracy theorists" to describe those who were incredulous to the rubber stamped conclusions of the Warren Commission, which was presided over by Chase Manhattan and Council on Foreign Relations Chairman John McCloy and CIA Director and Rockefeller cousin, Allen Dulles.

This label would be used to slander and shut down anyone who dared to contradict the Crown's increasingly outlandish versions of the nature of reality. Words like "misinformation" and "disinformation", which had previously been used only by intelligence assets to describe unruly foreign leaders, were now being bandied about to discredit intelligent researchers that opposed government policies to shut down democratic debate.

This violation of the First Amendment was taken to the extreme when, during the Covid-19 "Crown venom" suspension of our Constitution, scores of the most intelligent humans on the planet were "deplatformed" from the DARPA-net, including myself.

While truth was being censored, the Crown's ad agencies and Hollywood propaganda arm continued their great "reveal", doubling down on their efforts to debase humanity and scramble our language using one of the seven sacred sciences that their Nephilim ancestors had taught them could be used to control humanity – rhetoric.

Etymology is at the heart of all Crown language usurpation and inversion. In the hands of Tavistock propagandists, United Nations warmongers become "peacekeepers". Something really good becomes "sick" or "wicked". Eating chocolate becomes a "guilty pleasure". The epidemic of suicides, drug abuse, and kids falling behind in school due to draconian COVID lock-downs are blamed on "the pandemic". When the CIA overthrows a democratically-elected Ukrainian government, then slaps sanctions on Russia to punish them for responding, the economic pain we all feel is caused by "Putin's war".

With digital advances toward their Fourth Industrial Revolution, the Crown grew closer to achieving full spectrum dominance. Now they were coming out of the closet, attempting to initiate as many humans as possible into their Satanic cult. This would be pushed forward by economic shocks and a global austerity program. They called it The Great Reset.

In 1970, even before DARPA had unleashed its internet weapon, Alvin Toffler wrote his best-selling book, *Future Shock,* in which he predicted that in the near future, humanity would be confronted with such drastic changes in such a short time that it would put them into a state of shock. The sudden onslaught of computers, the internet, and social media has produced just such a state of affairs.

Adam and Eve had been lured out of the Garden of Eden by an Anunnaki serpent that encouraged them to eat from the Tree of Knowledge. That "knowledge" can be seen as the worship of one's own intellect at the expense of intuition, natural relationships, and reciprocity. It is no coincidence that the logo for Apple computers, one of the drivers of DARPA's Silicon Valley Luciferian agenda, depicts an apple with a bite taken out of it.

The bloodline had for centuries hidden behind both Catholic and Protestant religions, before using their Royal Societies to commandeer a fake science that they could use to justify their colonization and slavery. Recently, in another attempt to divide and conquer, their medium propagandists have pushed a narrative that science and religion are enemies of one another. Now we have seen that the Crown controls both.

But the people kept remembering. New scientists were rediscovering God in droves. Ironically, the DARPA net proved fruitful as a means to disseminate truth. Musk's Teslas kept running into cops parked on the side of the road. Only 12% of Americans had gotten their COVID-19 booster. To appeal to this great mass of remembering humanity, the Tavistock would have to come up with a hip new cover. They called it the Woke Movement.

Chapter 19

Manufacturing the Two-Party Cult

To create this new Woke Movement, the Crown first had to ensure that the political climate in the United States Corporation was right. President Barrack Obama won the election of 2008 and served two terms. Though many celebrated the election of America's first black president, Obama for the most part picked up where the Bushes and Clinton left off in handing America's sovereignty back to the Crown.

His accomplishments included the assassination of arguably Africa's greatest leader of all time, Libya's Muammar Gaddafi, the unleashing of Aga Khan's ISIS terrorists upon the socialist Republic of Syria, and the overthrow of democratically-elected governments in Ukraine and Honduras. There were claims that his father was a CIA agent in Kenya, a former British colony and part of the Commonwealth.

Obama was cozy with the Chicago School of Economics, which was founded by the Rockefeller Foundation and produced advocates of an economy based on laissez faire capitalism like Milton Friedman and George Stigler.

In 2016, Vermont's Independent Senator, Bernie Sanders, rode a wave of disgust with this failed neo-British mercantilism that had overtaken the US during the Reagan years, as he stormed to the lead in the Democratic presidential primary. Sanders railed against Wall Street banks and the super-rich. Voting irregularities occurred in dozens of states and eventually the corporate media and the Democrats alike rolled over and crowned Hillary Clinton their nominee.

But the Crown was alarmed by the sudden burst of democratic socialism that Sanders represented. People were remembering. The 2008 housing crash and the ensuing bailout of the world's largest banks had reminded people of the stranglehold which the elite had on their lives. So the spies at MI-6 scrambled to create a candidate who could channel this new wave of populism into an outcome that the bloodline could live with. That candidate was Donald Trump.

In 1987, Donald Trump purchased 93% of Resorts International, a CIA drug money laundry founded by Crown agents and cousins Allen Dulles and David Rockefeller as the Mary Carter Paint Company in the 1950s. A year later, Trump bought the Atlantic City, New Jersey, Taj Mahal Casino from Resorts International, then began buying up other properties on the Atlantic City boardwalk.

But Trump was in over his head and he soon declared bankruptcy. His main creditor was Rothschild Inc. In 1992, Wilbur Ross, later Trump's Commerce Secretary, struck a deal with Trump as head of Rothschild Inc.'s bankruptcy advisory team. Trump would relinquish control of 50% of the Taj Mahal and allow the Trump brand to be used by Rothschild Inc. as a cash cow and political tool. Before marrying future Trump senior advisor Jared Kushner, Trump's daughter, Ivanka, had been dating Lord Jacob Rothschild's son Nathan.

In 2013, Cambridge Analytica was spun off from British private intelligence company SCL Group to "participate in American politics". Its logo depicted a brain with vectors connecting dots. Its founder was Nigel John Oakes, who also founded SCL Group and the Behavioral Dynamics Institute, based in Jakarta, Indonesia.

Oakes had ties to the British royal family. In the 1980's, he had dated Lady Helen Windsor, daughter of Prince Edward, Duke of Kent. His father was Major John Waddington Oakes, High Sheriff of Warwickshire. The family was part of Britain's landed gentry and Nigel attended blue-blood stronghold Eton College. There he met

Alexander Nix, who after a fourteen-year stint at SCL Group would be tapped to head Cambridge Analytica.

SCL or Strategic Communication Laboratories also owned AggregateIQ which "participated" in Canadian elections from its Toronto base. SCL had close ties to the British royals, the British military, NATO, and the US Department of Defense. One of its directors was Lord Ivar Mountbatten, second cousin of King Charles III and godfather to Lady Louise Windsor, another daughter of Prince Edward.

SCL served as a psychological warfare contractor to both the British and US militaries in Afghanistan and Iraq. In the early 1990s, it began targeting elections in developing nations. In 2005, at the Defence and Security Equipment International trade show in London, SCL showcased its ability to "influence operations" and create "mass deception". So successful were its efforts that the parent company now called itself SCL Elections.

Cambridge Analytica insider Robert Mercer was an early pioneer in artificial intelligence and is a major funder of far-right US groups like Heritage Foundation, Cato Institute, Breitbart.com, and Club for Growth. He resides at Owl's Nest mansion in New York and was named as a director of eight different Crown-controlled Bermuda-based firms implicated in tax evasion by the Paradise Papers.

Around twelve minutes into a British Channel 4 undercover interview, Cambridge Analytica CEO Alexander Nix bragged about how both Cambridge and SCL, often using Israeli contractors, had secretly manipulated elections in over 200 countries around the world. They used bribes, Ukrainian prostitutes, and fake election cards.

It was later discovered that DARPA contractor Facebook had fed user information to Cambridge Analytica, which they used to steer the results of the 2016 presidential election in favor of their fake right-wing populist Donald Trump, who had been busy making the rounds on alt-right radio and podcasts proclaiming his willingness to take on the very establishment that was now rigging the election in his favor.

As Nix put it in his Channel 4 interview, "We just put information into the bloodstream of the internet, and then watch it grow, give it a little push every now and again... like a remote control. It has to happen without anyone thinking, 'that's propaganda', because the moment you think 'that's propaganda', the next question is, 'who's put that out?'.

The Crown knew that Trump was no populist. He staffed his entire cabinet with billionaires, cut taxes on corporations and the wealthy, and further deregulated the cartels. He cut off ties with the Palestinians and moved the US Embassy in Israel to Jerusalem, enraging the Muslim world. And he launched Operation Warp Speed to expedite the Crown's mass-vaccination eugenics program.

But the most important thing Crown agent Trump did was enrage liberals and progressives with his haughty demeanor. To many conservatives, tired of what seemed like a well-coordinated mob of "political correctness" enforcers on the "left", Trump was music to their ears. Trump would serve as a Trojan Horse through which GCHQ could divide its United States Corporation up into two seemingly different political camps that were controlled, like science and religion, by the same master.

Astute conspiracy researchers, largely based in the US, had exposed many of the Crown's machinations. And Bernie Sander's popularity among frustrated youth scared the bloodline. Authentic left-wing populism was always their greatest fear, so they would invert accepted political theory by creating the alt-right as the new "populist" bandwagon.

The bloodline's modus operandi had always been a stateless privatized global piracy that set out to crush any democratic participation. How could the alt-right offer any meaningful solutions to this, since they seemed to believe in the same ideology? The old Masonic credo, Ordo ab Chao (Order out of Chaos), was about to play out once again. The Crown had played its Trump card.

GCHQ monitored their Manchurian candidate and soon began to use him as a bad cop foil. Using a fake intelligence dossier from MI-6 agent Christopher Steele, Rep. Adam Schiff (CA), from the old Schiff banking family that intermarried with the Goldman Sachs and

Kuhn Loebs, accused Trump of colluding with Russia to steal the 2016 election from Hillary Clinton. Steele had run the MI-6 Russia desk from 2006-2009 before founding Orbis Business Intelligence, a private intelligence firm based in London.

Using Trump as a foil, anti-Russian propaganda reached a fever pitch not seen since the Cold War. But this time, it was the liberals crying for Putin's head. Deranged by Trump, these liberals, in another Crown-orchestrated inversion, came to love the CIA, the FBI, and the corporate media monopoly.

Anyone who pretended to oppose Trump was their new best friend. And Putin was now their worst enemy. Though the Steele dossier and later attempts to connect Hunter Biden's laptop to Russian disinformation both proved fallacious, the damage had been done. One of the Crown's main objectives is to keep Russia and the US at odds with each other because if these two heavily armed countries ever got together in opposition to the Crown, their days would be numbered.

While most progressives were caught up in this Tavistock-driven campaign of inversion, many conservatives eagerly jumped onto the QAnon bandwagon. QAnon is an extremely sophisticated intelligence operation being carried out by QinetiQ, a British defense technology firm. All these "Qs" likely stand for "Queen", who until her death in 2022, held the golden share in QinetiQ.

QinetiQ was launched in 2001 after British Defense Secretary Lewis Moonie privatized the Defence Evaluation and Research Agency. In 2003, the Carlyle Group took a 33% stake in the firm, but the monarchy maintains its golden share. The shady Carlyle Group, where President Bush Sr. and Sharif bin Laden alike had worked, is the world's largest private equity firm with over $400 billion in assets. It is also one of the world's largest defense contractors.

The Crown's DARPA social media contractors pushed disinformation out to both "sides" and America was soon on the verge of a civil war as the two Crown-manipulated cults warred with with one another. Of course, they didn't understand that their respective gurus were being handled by the same ancient bloodline.

In 2020, Senator Bernie Sanders again ran in the Democratic primary, garnering a similar groundswell of support. Again he was shut down by the corporate media just when it looked like he might win the nomination. Instead, the Crown marched out Obama's former Vice-President and long-time Delaware Senator Joe Biden to carry their agenda across the finish line.

Trump had divided the country like never before. Now they needed a compliant, or better yet, senile old man to preside over millions of vaccine deaths in his role as global hospice manager. And to serve as the frontman for their escalating attacks on Russia.

Biden descends from British and Irish lineage. Both William and Christopher Biden had been officers with the British East India Company. His state of Delaware had served as a quasi-offshore banking locale for tax-dodging Crown corporations for decades. While Obama's Vice President in 2016, Biden pressured newly installed Ukrainian President and chocolate billionaire, Petro Poroshenko, to fire a Ukrainian prosecutor who was looking into the illegal activities of Burisma, a natural gas firm in which Joe's son Hunter Biden was deeply involved. These activities allegedly included the construction of secret bio-weapons research labs in Ukraine.

Biden predictably chose California Senator Kamala Harris as his running mate. She is a descendant of Jamaican slave owner Hamilton Brown. Her husband, and now second gentleman of the United States, Doug Emhoff, was a partner at DLA Piper, the Crown's law firm in the US. He recently made his first public speech. It was well-televised and warned of a growing wave of anti-Semitism in the US. Emhoff claims Jewish heritage, but remember, anti-Semitism is not opposition to Jews or Israel. It is opposition to those who spoke a family of languages that suddenly appeared in the Middle East 8,500 years ago, at the exact same time as the Anunnaki intervention.

Amidst a swirl of election irregularities involving the voting machines of Lord Mark Malloch-Brown's Smartmatic and Dominion Resources, Biden won the election. On January 6, 2021, a well-organized crowd stormed the US Capitol. It was later revealed that many of its leaders were FBI informants. The event served to cement the divisions between the two arms of the Crown cult – Democrat and Republican. It also provided a new class of "domestic terrorists" going forward, ensuring a boom in contracts at Homeland Security.

The Biden Administration was quickly staffed with BlackRock alumni. With over $10 trillion under management, BlackRock is the world's largest asset manager. It is owned by the privately-held Vanguard. These two companies, which are actually one company, are the top two shareholders of nearly every single Fortune 500 corporation.

Vanguard and BlackRock are major repositories for Crown wealth, as the bloodline increasingly leans on private equity firms to conceal whatever wealth they are not holding in City of London/Bank of England offshore accounts. State Street Capital and Fidelity Management Resources (FMR) are also powerful Crown-controlled investment firms, nearly always appearing in the top five shareholders of Fortune 500 firms.

BlackRock was founded in 1988 from an initial investment by the Blackstone Group, which had just picked up numerous bankrupt Savings & Loans on the cheap following the CIA and mob-engineered S&L crisis. The names of these two firms are instructive. BlackRock was contracted by the US government to sort out the carnage after the 2008 financial meltdown that left AIG and Bear Stearns bankrupt. Their plan included handing Merrill Lynch over to Bank of America, Lehman Brothers to Barclays, Bear Stearns to JP Morgan Chase, and Wachovia to Wells Fargo. This resulted in the nation's twelve largest banks now controlling 70% of all bank assets.

Even before he made it to the White House, Biden's chief political strategist during his 2020 campaign had been Michael Donilan, whose brother Tom ran BlackRock's political think tank. Once Biden was elected, the BlackRock floodgate opened.

BlackRock executive Brian Deese would come to head Biden's National Economic Council. BlackRock founder and insider Larry Fink would become Biden's top economic advisor. BlackRock senior advisor Wally Adeyemo would become Deputy Treasury Secretary and BlackRock executive Michael Pyle would become the top economic advisor to Vice-President Kamala Harris. On December 14, 2022, Adeyemo was elevated to replace Fink as Biden's top economic advisor.

Chief among Adeyemo's tasks would be to advance the Environmental, Social, and Governance (ESG) agenda that had originated at BlackRock, Vanguard, and Goldman Sachs.

The Crown knew full well that the actual "woke" people were the ones who had already turned "Rothschild" into a dirty word, as they helped others remember what had happened to humanity and the earth throughout recent history.

Now, using another rhetorical sacred science inversion, they would ascribe the term "woke" to the burgeoning ranks of technological zombies, who were dutifully carrying their cell phones (ankle bracelets) everywhere they went, enabling these unwitting Crown minions to pummel truth-tellers caught in the worldwide web who didn't agree with the new BlackRock ESG social credit system. All the while these "woke" zombies were creating an environmental catastrophe as growing numbers of Amazon trucks ate up the pavement in order to satiate their never-quenched appetite for "woke" acquisition.

Chapter 20

Wokism and Hive Mind Singularity

Drunk with the worship of their newfound Google-derived "intellect", these new liberal-identifying Black Shirts spent their days excoriating anyone who wouldn't supplement their plentiful narcissism with total subservience to the new busily-censoring Google god. These phone-toting "phonies" didn't realize that they no longer had a brain to worship. They were simply repeating a script written by their DARPA handlers, whether it appeared on Facebook, Instagram, TikTok, or another social media intelligence operation. And the script was about to get even darker.

Just as the Crown had hidden behind its hand-picked black and brown administrators in the newly "independent" Commonwealth and global South nations, lauding "decolonization" as something they should be applauded for, they now attempted to coral their new zombie mind-controlled device carriers into a hive mind singularity that would advance the interests of the bloodline by activating the hive to shout down dissenters.

This fifth-generation (5G) weaponization of Project Monarch-derived techniques was now aimed not at a single subject, but at the whole of humanity.

"Equity" quickly became a buzzword for hive mind formation, but most phonies had no idea that this was financial terminology describing their monetization, and had nothing to do with equality.

The bloodline media feigned support for blacks, women, and

transsexuals, while blacks sank further into poverty, salaries for women remained stagnant, and the Crown's hospital cartel made a fortune castrating 15-year-old boys, and performing double mastectomies on teenage girls.

They promoted sexual confusion as a way to further invert natural law, introducing more and more pronouns that were to be used to describe one's sexual orientation. Drag queens started appearing at primary schools. Those who refused to use the pronouns or opposed the sexualization of children were shouted down as backward hillbillies who simply were not "woke".

The bloodline promoted trans-humanism for the exact same reason, using Royal Society member and spokesman Elon Musk to make it "cool". Musk's grandfather had earlier been a leader in the Canadian trans-humanist movement. Musk's Neuralink is developing a brain mesh interface to essentially wire humans and computers together. His Starlink is providing targeting for the Ukrainian military while blanketing the planet with 5G satellites.

Another plank of wokism was an open border policy. African and Middle East migrants flooded into Europe, mainly from countries that the Crown had decimated through its oil wars. The US border with Mexico was overrun by asylum seekers. Most were from Venezuela, Nicaragua, and Cuba where Bolivarian socialism, Sandinismo, and the Castro brothers had stood up to bloodline neocolonialism. Many were used by the CIA's Mexican drug cartels to transport the deadly new drug fentanyl, which is killing thousands of unsuspecting Americans.

Many of the migrants had been encouraged to come, receiving preloaded cash cards from George Soros' and Lord Mark Malloch-Brown's Open Society Foundation for the journey. Anyone who opposed the open border policy was deemed a racist, but the real white supremacists were the ones allowing these poor people to enter the US under the guise of their woke agenda to be used as cheap labor by Crown meat packers and agribusiness conglomerates.

As BlackRock pushed its ESG plan forward, the Li family dragons in China introduced a social credit system, using Google's Dragonfly software. The system punished those who refused to submit to mass vaccination programs or who criticized the government in any way. David Rockefeller once praised this increasingly draconian control system as "the China model".

Non-fungible tokens were introduced into the DARPA internet grid, as were cryptocurrencies. Billions were stolen from naive mostly young investors and funneled into Crown intelligence and smuggling operations. They were shaken down by hip Crown frontmen like Sam Bankman-Fried.

In late 2022, Bankman-Fried looted his company, FTX, to cash out his biggest shareholder just before declaring bankruptcy. The golden parachute went to Binance, a cryptocurrency exchange based on high-frequency trading technology that was founded in 2017 and is registered in the Crown's Cayman Islands off-shore haven.

In 2021, Binance had come under investigation by the US Department of Justice and the Internal Revenue Service for money laundering and tax crimes. That same year, the UK Financial Conduct Authority halted the operations of the company there.

Binance also operates offices in Malta and Jersey – two other important City of London-controlled offshore tax havens. They invested $500 million in Elon Musk's 2022 Twitter takeover. The biggest "investor" in Binance is Vertex Ventures, which is based in Israel, home to Crown CIA subcontractor Mossad.

Black-ops funding cryptocurrencies and blockchain technology serve as red herring gateways into a global 5G-driven electronic currency controlled by the City of London. A company called Digital Currency Group (DCG) owns the majority of the blockchain and cryptocurrency space.

DCGs website calls it, "...the epicenter of the bitcoin and blockchain industry". Former Treasury Secretary and New York Fed insider Larry Summers is an advisor to the DCG board, whose members include Lawrence Lenihan, Glenn Hutchins, and Barry Silbert.

Lenihan is a former IBM insider, who co-developed the company's first transactional interactive multimedia software kiosk products. He once served as chairman of the Duke University Pratt

School of Engineering Devil Venture Fund. He is also on the boards of Body Labs and TraceLink.

Body Labs is a software provider of human-aware artificial intelligence that understands "the 3D body shape and motion of people" from photos or videos. Lenihan provided start-up capital for Body Labs from his FirstMark Capital fund, which he started after his stint at IBM. FirstMark's focus is Big Data and AI. Body Labs was purchased by Amazon in 2017 and will play a key role in the development of body recognition software to be installed in 5G smart surveillance cameras.

TraceLink calls itself a "life sciences cloud" that specializes in "global track & trace", "global compliance", and "digital supply chain". They work closely with Big Pharma and the hospital conglomerates. TraceLink provides the technology used to track packages from production to point of sale and that same technology could certainly be adapted to "track & trace" human microchip recipients.

Glenn Hutchins is a member of the board of directors of the New York Federal Reserve Bank, which is by far the most powerful of the Fed branches. Hutchins is also a director at AT&T, which is rolling out its 5G Evolution business. Hutchins also co-chairs the Brookings Institute and is vice-chair of the powerful Economic Club of New York.

He also happens to be the co-founder of Silver Lake, which is a global leader in technology investing, with over $43 billion in combined assets. Its leadership consists of former investment bankers with Goldman Sachs, JP Morgan Chase, Credit Suisse, and Morgan Stanley. Its partners include NASDAQ, Motorola Solutions, Skype, Ancestry.com, Alibaba, Dell, Intelsat, and Tesla. It has bases in Silicon Valley, New York, London, and Hong Kong.

Hutchins is part owner of the Boston Celtics, a co-chair of Harvard's capital campaign, a board member at the Center for American Progress and the Obama Foundation, and a former board member at NASDAQ, SunGuard Data Systems, and Instinet. He is also on the Executive Committee at New York Presbyterian

Hospital, which is connected to the City of London-based Anglican Church.

In March 2005, Bill Gates met with Queen Elizabeth and the Duke of Edinburgh at Buckingham Palace where he received the title of Knight Commander of the British Empire. Gates would spend the next seventeen years carrying out a global eugenics-through-vaccination reign of terror that must have made his now-deceased patrons proud. In 1988, Prince Philip Duke of Edinburgh told Deutsche Press-Agentur (German Press Agency), "In the event that I am reincarnated, I would like to return as a deadly virus, to contribute something to solving overpopulation."

In March 2020, Knight Commander Gates called for a global tracking system to battle COVID-19. In September 2022, his Gates Foundation committed $200 million towards the establishment of a global digital identification system and civil registry, no doubt based on updating one's vaccines in order to grow the Knight Commander's bank account.

More ancient Masonic sayings were about to play out. Three Latin phrases appear on the Great Seal of the United States: E Pluribus Unum (out of many, one), Annuit Coeptis (he favors our undertakings), and Novus Ordo Seclorum (new order of the ages). The modern-day bloodline generals were calling it, The Great Reset.

Chapter 21

COVID-19 and The Great Reset

On November 20, 2018, US Patent Number 10,130,701 was granted to the UK-based Pirbright Institute. That patent was for coronavirus, which translates from Latin as "Crown venom". The Pirbright Institute runs biomedical research facilities located on 200-acres of land controlled by the British Ministry of Defense near the town of Surrey, England. It was in this region that mad cow, or Creutzfeldt-Jakob, disease broke out in 1986.

The Pirbright Institute has close affiliations with pharmaceutical multinationals, including the British Merial (a joint venture between the US drug company Merck and the French Sanofi-Aventis) and the German Boehringer Ingelheim. Funding comes from the Crown charity Wellcome Trust and the Bill and Melinda Gates Foundation, the two largest investors in vaccine research in the world.

Wellcome Trust was founded in 1936 by Sir Henry Wellcome who split his Burroughs Wellcome & Co. pharmaceutical empire into Glaxo Wellcome and the Wellcome Trust. Glaxo Wellcome merged with SmithKline Beecham in 2000 to become Glaxo SmithKline (GSK).

In 1891, Freemason Henry Welcome launched Columbia Lodge Mo. 2397 for the, "...welding of a new tie to the English-speaking people of the two hemispheres." This secret society carried forth the wishes of Cecil Rhodes last will and testament, serving as the planning group that created both the Business Round Table and the Pilgrims Society. The modern torch-bearer in this effort is the Atlantic Council.

During the 2nd South African Boer War, Burroughs Wellcome supplied vaccines to the British Army to conduct the first mass human vaccine experiments in concentration camps holding Boer prisoners. In 1909, Burroughs Wellcome funded the Pilgrims Society First Imperial Press Conference, which launched the Empire Press Union that eventually staffed both UK and US intelligence agencies.

African explorer Sir Henry M. Stanley, a friend of Cecil Rhodes, had been funded during his Congolese expedition by Burroughs Wellcome. He was also an agent of the East India Company. While taking over the Congo for Belgium, King Leopold collected poisons that he delivered to Burroughs Wellcome for the creation of their pharmaceutical empire.

Stanley's heirs own a castle near Pirbright. Lord Pirbright Henry de Worms, 1st Baron Pirbright was the great-grandson of Mayer Amschel Rothschild, who once stated, "I care not who controls a nation's government, so long as I control her currency."

Lord Pirbright, who had been born on a Rothschild tea plantation in Ceylon (now Sri Lanka), served Queen Victoria as Undersecretary of State for the Colonies from 1888-1892. Vaccine manufacturing began at the Pirbright in 1961, where a foot and mouth disease jab was created by Wellcome Foundation Ltd. Research.

On October 18, 2019, the Wellcome Trust and Pirbright Institute got together with the Gates Foundation, the World Economic Forum, the Rockefeller Foundation, and DARPA to fund Event 201 at Johns Hopkins University in New York City. The event was built using the Rockefeller Foundation's Operation Lockstep, which had been published in 2010. It laid out a scenario where a deadly coronavirus was unleashed upon the planet, then gamed how people would respond to heavy-handed government-mandated lockdowns.

One month earlier on September 17, 2019, interest rates on overnight repurchase agreements (repos) had spiked unexpectedly. The New York Federal Reserve responded by injecting $75 billion into the repo system every morning for the next week. There were rumors that Deutsche Bank, which had made a killing shorting airline and insurance stocks in the lead-up to the Crown's Securacom-orchestrated 911 event, was about to go under, taking the global stock exchanges with it. The economy needed a shock – a Great Reset.

It was no coincidence that on the very same day of Event 201, the 7th World Military Games commenced in Wuhan, China. From October 18-27, 2019, military athletes from 109 countries took part in the event. It was the first time China had hosted the event. To showcase the technological advances that the country had made with the help of Google and IBM, China deployed its first 5G system in Wuhan for the games.

Not far from the games, a group called the EcoHealth Alliance had been funding gain of function bio-weapon research at the Wuhan Institute of Virology (WIV). In 2014, WIV added a National Bio-safety Laboratory where it experimented on deadly viruses like SARS, Japanese encephalitis, and dengue. This endeavor was in close cooperation with the Galveston National Laboratory at the University of Texas and the National Microbiology Laboratory of Canada.

Founded in 1971 by British eugenicist Gerald Durrell as Wildlife Preservation Trust International, the group changed its name in 2010 to EcoHealth Alliance. It receives funding from DARPA, the Wellcome Trust, the Pirbright Institute, and Dr. Anthony Fauci's National Institutes for Health. Its partners include Johnson & Johnson, Boehringer-Ingelheim, King Saud University, Princeton University, Johns Hopkins University's Bloomberg School of Public Health, and the Brown University School of Public Health where Ashish Jha had served as Dean before taking temporary leave to become the White House Coronavirus Response Coordinator.

The first reports of a strange pneumonia-like virus had surfaced in Wuhan by December 2019. The Chinese Defense Ministry maintained that the US military had brought the virus to China during the World Military Games. US and UK health officials ignored these claims, then quickly dismissed any theories that the virus could have leaked from WUV, where EcoHealth Alliance had been conducting gain-of-function research. Instead, they claimed the virus came from either a bat or a pangolin being sold at a nearby wet market.

The two most vocal advocates of this theory were EcoHealth President and British zoologist Peter Daszak and Wellcome Trust Chairman Jeremy Farrar. In October 2019, the US government quietly shut down a program called PREDICT, which was supposed to detect global virus threats. And on April 24, 2020, the US NIH suddenly canceled funding to the EcoHealth Alliance.

From 1996-2013, Jeremy Farrar was Director of the Oxford University Clinical Research Unit in Ho Chi Minh City, Vietnam. In 2013, he was appointed Director of the Wellcome Trust. In 2023, he became Chief Scientist at the World Health Organization. He is a member of the Royal College of Physicians and in 2005, the same year Bill Gates was knighted, Farrar was bestowed the title of Officer of the Order of the British Empire. In 2015, he was elected a Fellow of the Royal Society. And in 2019 he was appointed Knight Bachelor.

By December 2022, the Pirbright Institute-patented coronavirus had killed 6.7 million people worldwide. Meanwhile, global economies were devastated by draconian government lockdowns as planned by Operation Lockstep and Event 201. Though markets initially swooned, a major stock market crash was avoided as small businesses shut down while "essential" Crown corporation businesses stayed open. An even greater consolidation of wealth was underway.

But this Great Reset was only partially economic in nature. The major component was depopulation. Crown pharmaceutical firms now jostled for position as President Trump's Operation Warp Speed relaxed regulations and liability for vaccine makers who would now combat the Pirbright's Crown venom with never-before-used mRNA vaccines. As of now, the public sector has no idea what these concoctions are made of. But it is clear that tens of thousands of people have already died from this additional dose of Crown poison.

There appears to be graphite in these bio-weapon shots. Graphite is extremely conductive and some think these shots will sync the people who get them with the ever-expanding 5G network, quite literally creating millions of human antennas to power the Crown Castle-built 5G system. Others think both the "virus" and the shots may consist of snake venom from the king cobra and the Chinese crate. This would give a whole new meaning to Crown venom. Interestingly, it would also add a physiological component to the initiation process whereby humans are not only being mind-controlled but possibly being genetically altered into the reptilian Anunnaki cult, as well.

Pfizer, Moderna, and EcoHealth Alliance partner Johnson & Johnson won the initial US vaccine sweepstakes. In 2002, the Gates Foundation purchased a large block of Pfizer stock. In 2013, Moderna, which works closely with the Crown's AstraZeneca, was awarded a $25 million grant by DARPA to develop mRNA vaccines.

Pfizer board member Scott Gottlieb served as head of sales, shilling as a doctor before the corporate media while pushing his Pfizer stock higher. Gottlieb is also a senior fellow at the American Enterprise Institute and former FDA Commissioner.

There was a systematic dumping of COVID-19 patients into otherwise perfectly healthy nursing homes. The eugenicists wanted to kill the weak and the sick. The bankers wanted to kill the creditors. The elderly, now retired and owed the social security and health care they had been paying into, fit both categories. The bloodline also realizes that elderly people, who were alive before the DARPA net was cast, are more suspicious of their ongoing Future Shock or Great Reset.

The coordinated government lockdowns also stunted the education of a whole generation of young children that were forced onto the DARPA net for instruction. People were also forced onto computers to shop and to work from home, as the big tech companies and their intelligence agency controllers attempted to bring in their cloud-based Fourth Industrial Revolution. Human batteries were being brought online to power the new electronic feudalism.

But the people continued to remember. By March 2022, people around the world finally stood up to the draconian lockdowns and vaccine mandates that their governments had unanimously imposed. Just as Covert Identification 2019 was being forced to an end by recalcitrant Canadian truckers, Russian troops invaded Ukraine to finally avenge the 2014 overthrow of the pro-Moscow Yanukovych government.

The new Ukrainian President was former movie star Volodymyr Zelenskyy. His movie and political career had been funded by Ukrainian oligarch Ihor Kolomoyskyi, whose Private Group controlled energy, steel, and chemical industries in Ukraine, Russia, the EU, Georgia, and Ghana. He was also the main shareholder at Burisma, the Ukrainian natural gas firm that was paying Hunter Biden exorbitant "consulting fees" and funding secret US bio-weapons labs in Ukraine. Kolomoyskyi had been banned from entering the United States in 2021, a year before Russia invaded Ukraine.

The US had been training Ukrainian paramilitary groups in Ukraine since 2014. Many have ties to the far-right pro-Nazi political parties Svoboda and Right Sector, including the Azov Battalion and the Kraken Regiment. These CIA-trained paramilitaries, funded in part by Kolomoyski, had been harassing and murdering Russian-speaking people in Eastern Ukraine. Russian President Vladimir Putin cited these attacks as the reason for his March 2022 invasion.

The US and their Royal Services Institute spokesmen immediately denounced Russia's move and announced a round of economic sanctions. These sanctions, while aimed at Russia, had a boomerang effect on Western economies, as oil markets skyrocketed, fertilizer shortages curbed global food production, and inflation set in around the world.

While Zelenskyy set about banning opposition political parties, media outlets, and even the Russian Orthodox Church; he was sold as a freedom-fighting Fauci-like saint by the fawning corporate media and Democratic politicians, who had been primed to be the new warmongers by the Trump/Russiagate psyop.

The greedy bloodline cartels raised prices at will. The Crown's oil giants rang up record profits. Chevron quadrupled its profits in the 1st quarter of 2022 to the highest it had seen for ten years. Biden Defense Secretary Lloyd Austin rewarded his former employer Raytheon with fat contracts to send Ukraine anti-missile defense systems. The Bretton Woods-backed US dollar strengthened. And people around the world, especially in the global South, scrambled to afford even basic food to eat. Famines began in Ethiopia, Madagascar, and Somalia, paving the way for yet more human depopulation. It was all part of the Great Reset.

Chapter 22

Stockholm Syndrome

If even half of what I have told you in this book is true, one could understand why many humans are so traumatized that they still refuse to remember what happened to us. Unfortunately, it is all true. And digesting this litany of insane psychopathic wetiko behavior from a single despotic and very much ruling bloodline is difficult.

Humans have been generationally abused by all the genocides, slavery, pillage, wars, plagues, religions, inverted science, and controlled media that these lizard-brain crazies have conjured up to keep us in line. There is no war crimes tribunal big enough to handle the total obliteration of natural law that has occurred at the hands of these unelected inbreeding tyrants.

The term Stockholm Syndrome came into use after a bank robbery in Stockholm, Sweden, in 1973. Four hostages were taken by the gunmen, Jan-Erik Olsson. But at the trial, none of the hostages would testify against him. They had developed a bond with their captor.

In the same way, many human beings, who once lived in accordance with relational and reciprocal natural law, have sadly become fond of their abusers. Instead of loathing the bloodline and its disconnected and ostentatious lifestyle, we covet it. In doing so, we grow less content and less grateful for all that Wakan Tanka has provided.

In the end, the fancy term Stockholm Syndrome can be boiled down to fear. Centuries of Crown terror have etched a deep-seated fear in the collective psyche of humanity. The nemesis of fear is love. Fear manifests as cowardice. Love translates into bravery.

The Crown' mediums, channelers, platformers, and programmers, who are all informed by researchers at the Tavistock Institute of Human Relations and DARPA, push out a steady stream of propaganda telling us the world is a dark, dangerous, and cynical place. This only serves to anchor and affirm the collective fear, which then manifests itself in society.

But like Malthus, Hobbes, Locke, and the rest, these modern-day Luciferian charlatans are simply projecting a worldview meant to justify the Crown's historical carnage. Now key servants of the Satanic cult, their twisted views of reality become even more morose. Eventually, they have no clue as to the nature of reality. They are completely sold out and broken.

Many in society, especially in the climber class, internalize the inverted morality of the bloodline. Instead of calling out a rich powerful person, they will blame that person's victim. Adages arise to justify this fear-driven cowardice in phrases like, "shit rolls downhill" or "the nail that sticks up gets hammered down".

Idiots, cowards, and people of low character are rewarded as they climb the Crown pyramid. To advance to a certain level of Freemasonry, the initiate is asked to spit on Jesus as he hangs on the cross. Those who refuse are commended for the decision and dismissed. Those who obey advance to the next level of this Satanic cult of Crown minions. It works the same in the corporate world. And sadly it now extends into non-profit and government sectors as well.

Even within families, the child that has gone out and made the most money or has the biggest house is often shown special favor by the parents. He or she is the golden child. Other children in the family that have gone their own way and retained their integrity and dignity by not becoming a cog in the Crown wage slavery consumption wheel, are often ostracized and treated badly by the parents. This morally inverted behavior has now been clinically diagnosed as acute narcissistic personality disorder. And it is rampant.

Many human beings have forgotten what it means to be human. Instead of saying, "Oh well, he's only human", we should say, "Too bad he's not human enough." These neurotic behaviors are not human, nor are they natural, as can easily be seen in any simple observation of nature. These are alien behaviors that contradict both natural law and humanity.

Banking is only the tip of the iceberg that is the Anunnaki bloodline control grid under which humans have, for the past 8,500 years, fallen under. Money is important as a tool to keep people climbing, acquiring, and in debt. Much more important to the Crown is perception management.

Some have argued that humans lack a third DNA strand that other animals have. Some say humans lack a Y chromosome, which other animals have. If either or both of these is true, did the Anunnaki intentionally alter humans in this way after their arrival to mute our power to perceive reality? I for one have learned far more from my cats and dogs than I have from any book or university.

The Crown learned through MK-ULTRA's Project Monarch that subjects (double meaning intended) could be brought to heel through the use of fear-based trauma, which would then disassociate the subject from ever "going there". It's the same method used by a child abuser to keep the kid quiet. And it has for a very long time been the main method of the bloodline to keep its subjects quiet.

What has changed is the sophistication of their methodology. This has everything to do with their 3rd and 4th Industrial Revolutions, which have produced a screen-based delivery system through which they can expand Project Monarch to reach virtually the entire population of the planet.

This has made it possible to deliver a certain uniformity in messaging, which is key to the creation of a hive mind singularity. Lately, they have pinned their hopes on hiding behind a message of wokeness. The only reason they had to do this is because a huge chunk of the global population was, in fact, waking up, or remembering. But not in the way they had hoped.

As with their George Soros-funded color revolutions, they got out ahead of the real awakening and inverted the meaning of the word "woke", which they then sold like dish soap through their social media intelligence agency subsidiaries. Their main goal in using this new ruse is to keep the conversation off of class or, worse yet, off of the Crown. In the meantime, they are dividing people along racial and sexual orientation lines. The more races and sexual identity pronouns they can come up with, the more ways they can divide people. It's pretty simple.

Just as it was with their Tower of Babel, the bloodline is attempting to invert and scramble the language so that we stay fearful, angry, and divided. In this hurried and harried state, humans cannot communicate about the real problem. And the royal Anunnaki bloodline and their Luciferian worldview, which they have spread around the world like the plague, is the real problem.

Google became god and people narcissistically worshiped their own Google-driven "intellects" at the expense of getting along. It was more important to be right about some minuscule fact than it was to be empathetic and try to see things from someone else's perspective, maybe actually learn something in the process.

They inundated us with screens and we began to worship imagery. Young men spent their days watching the Crown's pornography instead of asking a girl out on a date. "Selfies" were normalized. People couldn't go anywhere without taking a picture and posting it on social media. If the response to their narcissism wasn't sufficient, they would fly into a fit of rage or become despondent. The screens were capturing more than images. They were capturing souls. The Crown's British Telecom wing even produced an electronic implant for the eye called Soul Catcher.

The best thing humans can do is to turn off the Crown-controlled screens and go out into nature. You will notice right away that reality feels a lot more solid and comforting than the inverted virtual reality that the Crown's magicians project daily through our ankle bracelet devices and screens.

Fear has come to permeate society. This fear is, at its root, based on misperceptions about the nature of reality, lies that emanate from the bloodline aggressor. The mask has come off. With the introduction of a bio-weapon into the human population, and another bio-weapon to "cure" it, they have taken the old Masonic credo Ordo ab Chao (order out of chaos) to the next level. They have let us know that they wish to kill us. They have been forced out of the closet and have declared war on humanity.

If we are to respond in the proper way to this tangible threat to our very existence, we must first remember what it means to be human.

Chapter 23

The Great Remembering

It was five days before Christmas and 2023 was just around the corner. We got three feet of snow over the course of a week. A blizzard warning was issued and I-90 was shut down from Mitchell, South Dakota west to the Wyoming border. Then it got cold. Tonight the wind chill is forecast to drop to -55F. The yard light went out. It must have frozen. I shoveled snow for eight days in a row. Our shower froze. I was having a Florida moment.

I took Slow Loris for his morning walk. While he zoned in on the rosy finches hanging around the bird feeder, I noticed a herd of deer hustling up the hill across the road. Behind them, a large five-point mule deer buck waited and watched as the rest passed by and continued up the hill. When they had reached the top, three more deer ran quickly across the road and scampered past the buck on their way up. But still, he waited and watched. I did the same, becoming part of the herd for just a moment. The buck let me know that I was and thanked me. Then he trotted majestically up the hill behind those he loved and therefore protected.

The herd had huddled behind our apartment for four days, waiting out the snow. They used their perfectly designed hooves to dig through three feet of snow. At the bottom they found dry leaves to eat to get them through. I watched as the blizzard winds magically piled the snow on the hillside into the draws, clearing a path on the ridge for the herd to climb the hill. There, a pine forest awaited, which provided more forage and cover from the coming bitter cold.

It all seemed orchestrated by a maestro we could not comprehend. When I chose to become a part of the magic, I was welcomed by the protector of the herd. Liberal women would have seen the big buck as a dangerous pursuer of females, maybe even a male chauvinist. Conservative men would have objectified the buck and coveted his horns. Their perceptions having been poisoned by the Satanists. But I didn't care. I was too busy remembering to be bothered by Crown narratives designed to destroy my natural relationships.

I was comforted by the fact that many other humans were now also remembering. As I was writing this book, nearly every day I would stumble upon information some other researcher had dug up that either reinforced or added to my own. Many times before I had seen this synchronicity, where humans attempting to liberate their species and their planet from the bloodline worked in unison and at long distances from one another to come up with the exact same conclusions.

Today, for example, the Twitter files released by Elon Musk by progressive journalist Matt Taibbi in a show of political unity, tell us that the FBI was actually paying the salaries of certain Twitter employees as they censored anyone whose information destroyed the Crown's COVID-19 fairy tale. They were also providing Twitter with the names of people that they wanted to have banned from the platform. It was starting to look an awful lot like an electronic COINTELPRO – J. Edgar Hoover would have been proud.

In July 2022, someone blew up the Georgia Guidestones, a creepy American Stonehenge that recommended, among other things, a massive decrease in the world's population. The fraudulent potential war criminal, Anthony Fauci, was forced to resign his post as the head of the NIH, where his salary had been the largest of any government employee. Even Australia, where lockdowns were especially brutal, was forced to allow travelers in without a COVID jab.

When we do this work, we get help from Wakan Tanka. Despite the attempts to ostracize and isolate us, our lives just keep getting better. Meanwhile, those who cower and climb the Crown ladder see their lives get worse, as they often hide behind alcohol to justify their cynical worldview while their health and family relationships deteriorate.

The animals, trees, mountains, rivers and lakes, as well as the sky and the sun, are all willing to help any time we ask. But we have to first remember that we can literally communicate with them, despite the Tower of Babel and DARPA net attempts to end these exchanges.

To remember, we must spend more time in nature and away from the artificial constructs of the bloodline. We are animals, not aliens. Our relationship with this planet runs much deeper than the Anunnaki realize. They don't have the reciprocal connection that humans have with other creatures, plants, and stones because they are foreign to this planet. Neither they, nor their artificial intelligence (AI), are from here.

This explains why it seems like everything they do has to have the destruction of life on earth as its goal. They hate themselves, they hate humanity, and they hate this earth. It is for this reason that they are indeed synonymous with devils.

But Wakan Tanka is much more powerful than these devils. No matter how much carnage these insane wetiko invaders leave in their wake, the earth always bounces back. As an environmentalist, I've always been amazed at how quickly a clear-cut grows back or a stream cleans up after decades of abuse at the hands of some Crown timber or mining cartel.

Wakan Tanka allows this destruction to occur because not enough humans have remembered who we are. The minute enough do, as the Australian aborigines say, "the rocks and sticks go in the ground". A Great Flood or an Ice Age may occur. Or a meteor may strike the planet as Creator purges it of evildoers while leaving a remnant of indigenous earth people to try again to get enough people to remember so that this vicious Lucifer-driven cycle can stop.

If we learn from these wise humans, we can return to the Garden of Eden.

But the intergalactic bloodline parasites have thus far also left a remnant. And instead of listening to the wise hunter-gatherer remnants, humans have listened to the deceptive Serpent. We have chosen discontent and restlessness over utopia. We have chosen the illusion of intellectual prowess over relationships. We have chosen to forget rather than to remember.

A few years back my wife and I embarked on a trip through Thailand, Cambodia, Vietnam, Laos, Malaysia, Indonesia, Singapore, Australia, and New Zealand. One day, we set out to hitchhike from Darwin to Kakadu National Park. It was a long day with very few suspicious Aussies willing to pick us up.

We finally made it there and spent the rest of the day looking around the park. It was beautiful, but we didn't see a single animal the entire day. Somewhat dejected and exhausted, we decided to take the bus back to Darwin in the late afternoon.

Seated across from us was an aboriginal park ranger and her daughter, who I am guessing was four or five years old. The woman exuded a calm acceptance that I had not felt from a human being in quite some time. At some point during the trip, I busted out some snacks that we had bought. I noticed the child watching us as we ate, so I asked her mother if it was okay if I gave her some. The mother smiled and said it was. When I gave the little girl the whole bag, her eyes lit up. Her tiny hands could barely hold onto it.

For the next few minutes, we communicated without speaking, sending good energy back and forth. It was obvious that she had not had a white person treat her this way in a while, either. I let her know how much I respected her remnant clan, who believe that they sang the world into existence along a series of song lines that they use to walkabout to this day. She let me know that she felt this respect and appreciated it far more than the snacks I'd given her child.

When the child had finished the bag of chips, she began grabbing my arm, sitting on my feet, and doling out her own dose of loving affection. Almost immediately after that, communication hit its crescendo and wildlife began appearing outside the window of the bus.

First, we saw three wallabies, then a jabiru, then green and red parrots appeared, followed by some cockatoos. I settled into a Dreamtime state of absolute bliss, as once again I remembered the nature of reality. We had vibed the animals into appearing with our reciprocal kindness. They just wanted to be part of our herd, if only for a moment. They were now the ones reciprocating.

I was lucky. I had grown up in the land of Crazy Horse. My father was close to the Lakota people who lived on the Northern Cheyenne Reservation 50 miles west of our ranch. When I was a child, he would take me to the reservation to hunt antelope and grouse. He was one of the few whites the Lakota would allow to hunt on their land because they knew he respected them.

From early on in my life, I was given many opportunities to remember. I studied Lakota philosophy from a Sioux professor at the University of South Dakota, where I learned about the Sacred Hoop of life and that Indians had no desire to be capitalists and make money off the work of others.

The Lakota are also a remnant people. Their understanding of reality far precedes the Anunnaki intervention. They, like the Australian aborigines, know that the world does not exist in straight lines, but in circles involving relationships and reciprocity. It was from them that I learned to be semi-nomadic. It is better for the soul because it is how we were meant to live and how we did live before the Great Enslavement. Now, I was about to complete a major circle in that semi-nomadic life. I was going back to where it all started. I was going home.

Chapter 24

Slow Loris Returns to the Land of Crazy Horse

The day we found out that we had finally sold our self-sufficient 40 acre farm in the Missouri Ozarks, we had no idea where we were going. We just knew we had to end our farming days, which had begun in Elmo, Montana, twenty-five years earlier. I had grown up farming and worked for other local farmers after my father was killed in a car accident in 1978. At age 55, I knew that if I didn't do something different, my already ailing back would never recover.

Early on I saw the storm coming, which has now descended upon humanity. For this reason, we had chosen not to have children. And for this same reason, I had never used my Master's Degree to become a cog in the Crown's wage slave consumption wheel. We wanted to become self-sufficient and the only way to do this was to move to the country and buy land that we could work to produce or own food. I knew it wasn't perfect, but it was the best option we had within the rigged system to stay human. So that's what we did.

But I was tired of owning stolen land that I didn't really own. And I was tired of settling for agriculture as the means to getting free. I had already known that it was the biggest mistake humanity had made when we ceased to be semi-nomadic hunter-gatherers and became sedentary agriculturalists.

This time Wakan Tanka intervened with a friendly nudge through my sister, Kari. She owned a cabin in the central Black

Hills that she rented out to tourists in the summer. Since it was November and the cabin was empty, she said we could stay there a while. We went with the sacred nudge and set out with our adopted son – and my role model – Slow Loris, to return to the land of Crazy Horse.

The forest road to my sister's cabin was icy and I knew right away we couldn't stay there for the winter. We decided we would find a place in either Hot Springs or Spearfish, instead. There was a tourist brochure on the coffee table at the cabin that described how both the Northern Cheyenne and the Lakota people would winter at Hot Springs, where they could soak in the naturally warm mineral waters while camping beside the steaming Fall River. I went with that nudge from Wakan Tanka, too.

After three nights at my sister's cabin, we drove south into the southern Black Hills. We found a place to land that afternoon in Hot Springs. Our little cabin was two blocks from Evans Plunge, an indoor pool with steam room, hot tubs, and water slides, all fed by the famous natural hot springs. We bought a one-month pass and walked down the hill to the pool every day to start to heal our over-farmed bodies.

Towards the end of December, I saw an ad for a rental in Spearfish. Hot Springs had treated us very well, but it was a smaller town than Spearfish, which we had loved when we spent six months there in 2011. That time, we stayed at a weekly motel called the Royal Rest. The place was run by Dave Ovitz, a radical right-wing Constitutionalist. We argued and debated the nuances of left and right. In the end, we became very good friends.

I lost touch with Dave after we bought our farm in Missouri. But as I glanced at the ad for the Spearfish rental, I realized the contact number was Dave's, which I still had. So I called him up. After catching up, he told me he had bought the Royal Rest, but that it had gotten pretty run down. He told me that he was also managing a place just outside city limits at the mouth of Spearfish Canyon.

I knew the place and remembered thinking what a nice location it was during our first stay in Spearfish. I told him to save us a room and that we would arrive on New Year's Day, 2020. Wakan Tanka had nudged us again and we listened. On January 1st, we drove to the northern Black Hills and settled in Spearfish. We've been here for three years now.

Spearfish had expanded its trail system in our absence and the place we came to live was at a major crossroads. We can walk one block and be on a trail that heads out in three different directions. We bought some bikes and began hiking as many trails in the Black Hills as we could find. We got stronger and healthier.

I found a good chiropractor named, Scott Hourigan, who expanded on the therapeutic value of Hot Springs and straightened out my back. We felt we had taken the right fork. We were walking on the Good Red Road.

The news began to talk of a killer virus that had made its way to the US from China. By February, my WordPress Left Hook blog had been deleted, along with its millions of followers. Two weeks later, our bank account was frozen. It turned out that the bank was a subsidiary of the Crown's General Electric conglomerate.

Every other state in the US declared a COVID state of emergency, giving them the right to restrict people's movements. But my home state of South Dakota, led by Governor Kristi Noem, was the only one that refused to do this. Spearfish State Representative, Scott Odenbach, sponsored a bill that would ban COVID-19 vaccine mandates. And my new chiropractor, Scott Hourigan, led protests against those mandates in the state capital of Pierre.

Life through the "pandemic" was normal here. Walmart was the only business to require masks for entry. That lasted about a week, as hundreds of people, including myself, refused to wear one and walked right past the mask police and into the store. As much of the nation became enamored with the evil elf, Saint Fauci, people here were disgusted at the sight of his lying mouth opening.

With every passing day, it became clear why Wakan Tanka had nudged us to this place at this time. The stubborn common sense of the people of my home state soon wore off on governors in Florida, Georgia, Texas, Iowa, and Nebraska and rescinded their lockdowns.

Canadian truckers joined the party and took on even more draconian vaccine mandates in their Commonwealth country.

In the spirit of Crazy Horse, we had shouted the wetiko down and freed the world's people from martial law. Now we set out to expose the perpetrators. When we did, good things began to happen. Mossad agent Jeffrey Epstein, who funded numerous creepy high-tech projects at MIT was arrested for his pedophile ways. He was later "murdered" in prison before he could talk.

Epstein's handler was MI-6 agent Ghislaine Maxwell, whose spy father Robert Maxwell had cavorted with the Windsors before mysteriously disappearing from his yacht in the Mediterranean, was indicted for her role in recruiting underage girls to be abused by the bloodline elite. It was revealed that both Presidents Bill Clinton and Donald Trump had flown on Epstein's corporate jet.

Within weeks of Maxwell's indictment, her good friend Prince Andrew was forced to settle with Virginia Roberts Giuffre, who had accused the Duke of York of sexually abusing her when she was seventeen years old as part of the Maxwell bloodline pedophile ring. He paid Giuffre $17 million and was stripped of his royal duties by Buckingham Palace. But he was quite noticeably never arrested.

Interestingly, the Duke of York had been implicated in the scandal in November 2019, just before the Crown venom was released upon humanity. In early 2020, Prince Harry announced that he and his wife Meghan Markle were leaving the royal family to live in the US. Their new series on Netflix has just been released. It talks about the racism that Meghan endured from the Crown. Who knows what else they will reveal.

With the commencement of its COVID-19 depopulation program, the Anunnaki royal bloodline made its choice. They came out of the closet and exposed themselves, hoping they could escape imminent economic collapse and increasing royal scrutiny while overwhelming people with their wicked deception and getting them to join their "woke" Satanic cult.

But the Crown has always underestimated humanity. They could never imagine the fortitude, integrity, and character of the human race because they do not have these traits. Rather than joining their cult, many human beings have chosen instead to heed the advice of Lakota warrior and medicine man, Crazy Horse.

Like any good hunter, they continue to encourage the bloodline to continue exposing itself from its lair until they can get a good enough shot. The prey has emerged from its dark hole, the shots are flying, the fur is flying, and we real human beings are settling in for a long war with these interplanetary interlopers. We don't care if we live or die fighting this war. We just care that we win. It's what Wakan Tanka demands of us.

Love is the nemesis of fear. And I for one love my planet and my people way too much to allow this abuse to continue. So, Hoka Hey! Onward towards the danger! For, as my neighbor and superhero Crazy Horse once said, "It is a good day to die".

The bitter cold was followed by an amazing few days and nights of chinook winds. At 4:00 AM, we heard a "woosh". Our shower pipes had unfrozen. My Florida moment had passed. The yard light came back on. A large, dangling branch on the ash tree out front, which had hung precariously close to our car, dropped harmlessly in the wind the day we went to Rapid for Thai food and a movie. Within a few days the chinook had melted most all of the snow.

That evening, I saw the deer crossing the road again as they headed up the hill for the night. This time, there were two younger bucks with them acting as sentinels. The old buck crossed with the does and was heading up the hill with them. He had done his time. I joined the young bucks in a triangle formation to watch for cars. Everyone crossed safely just before dusk.

ABOUT THE AUTHOR

Dean Henderson is a world-renowned political analyst, historian, and author of seven books, including his best-seller, *Big Oil & Their Bankers in the Persian Gulf*. Among the early truth-tellers to be ghosted and deplatformed by social media giants like Facebook and Twitter, Dean's Left Hook blog had millions of views when it was deleted by the NSA in 2014 and again in 2019. Despite decades of threats and harassment, Henderson has never wavered from his life-long commitment to revealing the evils of the worldwide oligarchy.

Raised on a multi-generational farm in South Dakota, Dean's politics were influenced by the Farm Crisis in the 80s and a trip to war-torn Nicaragua with Witness for Peace in 1985. He earned a Bachelors degree from the University of South Dakota and a Masters Degree from the University of Montana, where he began writing as a columnist for the *Montana Kaimin* and married his wife Jill.

A rebel from an early age, Dean took part in many political and social actions during his college days, summing up his views with hard raucous jabs at the reigning oligarchy of the day in his radical "zine", *The Missoula Paper*. In 2004, Dean won the Democratic primary for Congress in Missouri's 8th District and a year later published his first book, *Big Oil & Their Bankers...*

In 2018, he delivered a speech entitled *All Roads Lead to the City of London* as part of the Confronting Oligarchy: Resisting Full Spectrum Dominance panel at the Deep Truth Conference in New York City.

Over the course of his 30-year career, Dean's work has been published in hundreds of print and online magazines and websites including *Multinational Monitor*, *In These Times*, *Paranoia*, *Info Wars*, Save the Males.ca, Global Research.ca, Zero Hedge, Naked Capitalism, Rense Radio, Tactical Talk with Zain Khan, The Richie Allen Show, David Icke's Ickonic, Press TV, RT News, Russia Channel 1, The Syria Times. His books have been translated into German, Russian and Turkish.

MORE BOOKS BY DEAN HENDERSON

BIG OIL & THEIR BANKERS IN THE PERSIAN GULF
Four Horsemen, Eight Families and Their Global Intelligence, Narcotics and Terror Network

Big Oil exposes a centuries-old cabal of global oligarchs who control the global economy through manipulation of the world's central banks and control of the planet's three most valuable commodities: oil, guns and drugs.

THE GRATEFUL UNRICH
Revolution in 50 Countries

Henderson's travelogue asks the hard social, political, and economic questions as he discovers himself, humanity and revolutionary politics through meeting God's chosen people.

STICKIN' IT TO THE MATRIX

Stickin' it to the Matrix is the modern version of Abbie Hoffman's *Steal This Book*. Funny and irreverent, the book is a practical guide to escape and extract from the matrix constructed by the global elite.

THE FEDERAL RESERVE CARTEL

A well-documented history of the privately-held US central bank which is largely controlled by eight families.

ILLUMINATI AGENDA 21
The Luciferian Plan to Destroy Creation

Co-written with his wife Jill Henderson, *Illuminati Agenda 21* follows the destructive trail of Luciferian hegemony from ancient Sumeria to the City of London which threatens to strip us of our humanity, replace us with machines and destroy Creation through technology.

NEPHILIM CROWN 5G APOCALYPSE

Nephilim Crown 5G Apocalypse is an indictment of the computer revolution as the latest mechanism through which royal bloodline families seek to control humanity. Since their intervention in Sumeria, these hybrid fallen angel Nephilim have usurped, steered, and plundered all of Creation as self-appointed god kings. The coming 5G apocalypse represents a great unveiling of not only their nefarious 5G deception, but of the fraudulent Nephilim Crown itself.

Printed in Dunstable, United Kingdom